THOR'S TRAVELS

Adventures of an American Jack Russell in Europe

Vienna, Austria, 2011

By Alex Starke

FIVE JACKS
PUBLISHING

Published by Starkewerks
in Eugene, Oregon USA

ISBN 978-0-9862909-0-9

Cover and book design by Anne Starke

ACKNOWLEDGEMENTS

To Thor, who dictated everything to me. The best companion anyone could ever dream of.

This book is dedicated to my wonderful wife, Anne. The best supporter, greatest critic, major cheerleader, and best friend one could have in life. I am a lucky man!

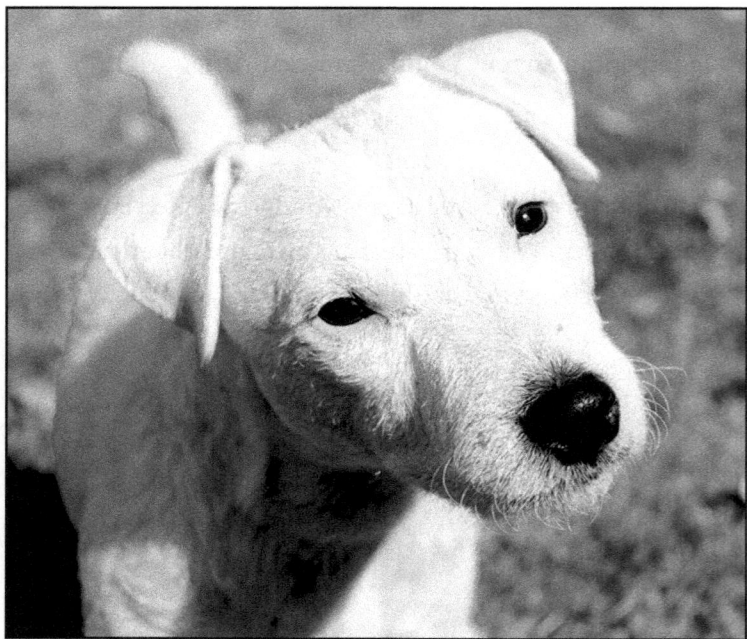

CHAPTER 1

Hello there! My name, if you haven't already guessed, is Thor. I have a few nicknames as well, such as Teddy Bear, Big Guy and a couple of others that I sometimes respond to. My favorite, though, is The Dude. I think it suits me rather well.

I will also interject a couple of stories as we go along that I feel are important. Anyway, since we've just met and before I begin to tell my little tale, let me give you a little background on my family and me.

There are four of us Jack Russells in our little pack, including me. I have two sisters, Daisy and Lily, who for the most part I adore, well, Daisy at least. Lily can be quite the young terror at times, but I do enjoy some good games of chase with her. I also have a younger brother whose name is Pippin, but I usually think of him as Pipsqueak. Pip can be a real pain sometimes, especially when he thinks he can take the top-dog spot from yours truly. It seems I have to set him straight at least once a day by giving him some growly teeth, followed by my rear end in his face. You'd think the nincompoop would learn.

Alex and Anne are our two human parents and round out the pack. I love Anne and Alex dearly and it shows in the way my tail vibrates and how I hold my ears at a certain angle. Dad (who I also call the Chief) is more gruff and direct to the point with us Jacks, while Mom is just the most sweetest and kindest to us all. She has taught all of us a few little tricks which we gleefully perform for her, mainly because we love her and we also know she will reward us with delicious treats. Together they make the best pack leaders a Jack could hope for. All in all, I have a pretty darn good family, in spite of the youngsters, Pippin and Lily, with their shenanigans.

As for me, I'm a very mellow Jack Russell as far as our particular breed goes. I know you wonder how that can be, but trust me, I am a laid-back kind of guy. Let's just say I don't go all bonkers when a squirrel or crow has the unmitigated audacity to invade our backyard. My sisters and brother are a totally different story. When they sense the impudent intruders they go blasting out the doggy-door at full throttle barking like there is no tomorrow.

Sometimes, in their frenzied attempt to be first out, all of them hit the door at once. I find it quite amusing to behold that sight. Picture if you can a struggling mass of nub-tailed posteriors trying to squeeze through an opening meant for one. Eventually one of them pops through, which causes the others to tumble outside like a gaggle of yapping and barking circus clowns. Not me, I'm on to the whole game and save my strength for the good stuff, like nice long walks, a game of tug, or my most-hallowed obsession, fetching the ball.

You humans may not know this, but we Jack Russells – in addition to being very smart – are very perceptive and quite sensitive to human emotions and thoughts. I really have this knack in a big way, so I can tell when Alex is ready to let me take him for a stroll. If he doesn't seem to be getting it I let him know with little grunts and whimpers – that always does the trick.

Now you may think you've seen a dog walk his Dad or Mom before, but let me tell you, when you've seen me and my bouncy little trot and smiling face, your whole day is going to brighten up considerably. Not that I'm bragging, but I can see it on the faces of people we pass, they always give a smile and I can sense the spreading warmth in their souls.

When I meet someone I particularly like, I charm them instantly with my tail vibrations and what Mom calls "hitch-walk." That walk happens when I am very excited and is comprised of me folding my ears back very cutely and doing a sort of rear-legged half lift while stepping in a circle. Well, you have to see it to really know I guess, but believe me it has an effect on humans like a super-charged good humor elixir. Truly I believe it is my mission in life to spread joy and happiness wherever I go – it's a mission that I embrace with all of my heart.

I think I might have mentioned before that I have a great affinity for that ball. Dad will give me all different kinds of throws, all of which I eagerly chase down. My very favorite, though, is the fast long grounder that takes a high bounce so I can jump up and catch it in mid-air! Boy do I love those, they really get my blood flowing. Daisy also joins in the fun and fetches her own ball with incredible acrobatic grace. Pipsqueak, the blockhead, has a rubber ball that he will occasionally give to Dad and allow him to throw, but usually he just rolls around on the grass with the thing. What a waste of ball time! Lily is good for maybe a few fetches, but then she gives up out of boredom. Sometimes the little upstart will try and get my ball away from me, which is untenable. The Dude's ball is sacred and he will not share it! To tell you the truth I think I could play ball all day long if the Chief would be willing to, but it seems he gets worn out after about an hour or so.

During the summer Dad brought in a small horse trough for us to dive into when we got too hot chasing the old ball. Ahh, nothing like a nice cool dip to revitalize the Dude for more game time. I always jump out, trot over right next to the Chief and give myself a vigorous shake off. It's my way of showing my appreciation by keeping him cool too.

One of my favorite duties is when Dad goes out for his errands during the day. I am his sharp-eyed navigator in the truck, and I also walk him around most of the stores he visits. My brother and sisters are pretty jealous of these journeys out with Dad and love to vocalize their displeasure. When we go out the door and hop into the truck, I can always be sure to hear the howls of anguish and outrage echoing from inside the house. Ha, as if they would know how to behave in a hardware or pet store anyway.

There are some occasions when all of us Jacks get to go somewhere in the truck – usually when we go up for a day hike or camping in the mountains. When we get ready to depart my siblings all burst out the front door and leap into the truck yapping, squealing, and squirming the whole time. They fairly trample poor Mom in their efforts to get next to the window or have the prime position on her lap. I always try to maintain my composure and dignity in spite of their boneheaded antics.

I have to admit though sometimes their utter excitement rubs off on me and I get a little wild.

In the evenings we all usually end up doing a little television viewing. My siblings and I love it when Mom and Dad watch a nature show. It makes for a fun-filled time complete with lots of barks and growls at all of the strange animals we see on the big screen. It is too bad the Chief and Mom won't let us get right up there at the television to get some good sniffs.

All of us get pretty impassioned if we see our archenemy, the fox, calmly trotting across the screen affecting total indifference to us. Where's the respect, I ask? It is very bewildering when Mom and Dad tell us, a bit loudly, to quit jumping up at the big screen. After all we just want to get in there and run that dastardly fox down the road a bit. I have to say that sometimes Mom and Dad can be so difficult!

At bedtime, all of us Jacks hop in beside Mom and Dad. The others are always jockeying and jostling for positions during the night, but not me, my spot is always next to the Chief. There are times though, that I do slip over to Mom's side for a night's cuddle. I have to make sure she knows I love her too, you know.

But I guess I am running on a bit too much. You're all here to get my travel story and I think I have a pretty good tale to tell, so let's get going!

CHAPTER 2

Things started to get very odd around the house in late summer. Alex began talking to Anne like a manic squirrel who had just discovered a huge horde of nuts in his tree. From what I could discern it was about going to somewhere called Vienna. He went on and on about how it would be great fun to go to this place during Christmastime. I had rarely seen him go on like this about something; he had a look in his eyes like my sister Daisy gets when you say the world "crow." He didn't go rocketing out the doggy-door though. Instead he turned around pointed at me and said, "We're going take you too, Dude!"

Well I'm always up for a trip, especially if it gets me out of the house for a few days. Like I said before, usually when we went somewhere it was camping. I always liked camping up in the mountains sleeping in a tent and waking up early to pursue chipmunks or the occasional bird. My three siblings and I really enjoyed sitting around the campfire at night, bravely barking at anything we heard out there in the dark. Unlike the camping trips, though, I was pretty sure the Chief had said that I was going to be the only one to go. So yeah, I vibrated my nub of a tail, cocked my head at him and thought, 'Sounds good to me Chief!'

But Dad wasn't done talking yet. He went on about some

of their previous trips – which were all before I was on the scene – to a place called Austria. From what I could glean, it seemed that Vienna was a city in Austria. It seemed to me he rambled on for hours about the sights and beauty of Vienna and Austria. I sure didn't know where these places were, but they sounded pretty nice to me.

Dad said one thing that jumped out at me. On one of those trips, while bicycling along a river called the Danube, they had stopped in a small village to spend the night at a small inn. The landlady had a little Jack Russell female that Mom and Dad immediately made friends with. As they stroked the little one, it reminded them of how much they missed their dogs back home. They thought wistfully of how nice it would be to have at least one of their furry kids traveling with them. Aha! Things were becoming clearer!

So they both decided to include me, The Dude, on this new trip. The Chief said one of the main reasons I was going was because I am very laid back. No argument there, Chief. He said I take in new situations with ease, and basically don't freak out in any scenario except when it is time for ball, of course. So true, so true. I tell you, the Chief is very perceptive at times, kind of like a big Jack Russell who doesn't know how to cock his head right. Pretty quickly after he said I was coming along, Dad got down to what he called "the research."

What I didn't know about research was that it meant that the Chief would be spending hour after seeming hour squinting at the computer getting information. Mostly it was about the paperwork he said I would need to travel and also where we were going to stay in Vienna.

I don't want to try and give you all the particulars of what he did, because I really didn't understand all of it. Truthfully, all of it made my little head kind of spin. I can tell you that the Chief will either put it out as a short book or place the information on my webpages. Yeah, I've got my own pages on the computer now, imagine that.

One thing that I do know about was that – in addition to all of the paperwork Dad collected – I had to get another rabies shot and something called a microchip so I could travel to Vienna. I'll fill you in on that painful experience in a little bit.

Mom and Dad talked a lot about how to get to Vienna. Me, I wondered why we just didn't get in the truck and drive ourselves. In the end Mom and the Chief decided that they were going to ride with somebody named Lufthansa who would drive us to Vienna. Mom said Lufthansa was who they went with on their previous trips to Vienna and that she liked him a lot. She also said Lufthansa was really friendly to traveling dogs and took good care of them during the journey. I didn't know who this Lufthansa guy was, but I was glad he liked dogs.

One day the Chief got off the computer and told me and Mom that he had found us all a place to stay in Vienna that allowed dogs. I wondered why this thing about allowing dogs or being dog-friendly was such an issue. I personally think that all establishments should allow dogs to visit their premises – except maybe that ill-mannered, chattering Chihuahua who lives across the street from us. I believe most dogs add a great deal of joy and character to anyplace they go. Why anyone would think differently baffles me, that's for sure.

CHAPTER 3

As I said before, I was definitely up for a trip, the thing was it didn't happen right away like most of our getaways. It seemed to me Dad was now hunched in front of that computer for even larger parts of the days and evenings doing his research. His behavior was infringing on my ball time, which, in my mind, was a grave injustice. I had to really give him an earful of grunts and whimpers to let him know the Dude needed to pursue the round bouncy object. I began to consider that infernal computer as some sort of inanimate rival and often thought of giving it a little chew when nobody was watching.

Eventually Dad's antics on the computer got back to a more normal routine. This was very gratifying for me as it resulted in more throwing and fetching of the coveted spherical object. I even forgave the computer its transgressions. Soon I began to forget that we were going anywhere.

After a few more weeks had gone by, though, I began to hear Vienna and Christmas again. When Dad said those words I could detect prodigious amounts of excitement radiating out of him. To me the effect was like a brilliant sun breaking out of the clouds on a gray day – my fine-tuned senses were almost blinded. Of course I would always just flash my winning smile at him, thinking, 'Slow down, Dad, before you blow a gasket or something.' Even Mom had to get on him every so often and tell him to calm down. I could tell something was coming, and I hoped I was going like it.

One day in late September the Chief arrived home carrying a puzzling contraption. It appeared to be a long black bag with a bunch of zippers and mesh sides that had a shoulder strap. My first thought was that Dad had gotten himself a fancy new suitcase or something and wanted to show it to me. I couldn't have been more wrong about that idea. I was soon to discover after he zipped open the top that he wanted me to get into the bag. I looked up at him thinking, 'Have you taken leave of your senses, Chief? Why in the world would I want to place myself inside a bag?' It would be humiliating, especially with Pippin and Lily watching me. There was no way this Dude was going into that bag – I was going to hold the line on this one!

But, you know, sometimes the Chief can be a devious son of a she-dog, because from inside of that bag he produced as if by magic a smaller bag that held my favorite jerky treats. Well, there was nothing more for it, my unwavering resistance melted in an instant and, as quickly as my brother Pip can chase a squirrel up a tree, I was in the proverbial bag.

Dad began to do the bag thing with me daily and sometimes drive around with me in the truck when I was inside of the zippered gadget. I didn't care for that much, as it was downright impossible to get sniffs from the window, let alone hang my head out in the breeze. One good thing was that there were treats, and we usually ended up at the dog park for a little game of fetch.

After a relatively short amount of time, I came to really

look forward to seeing that bag come out. As soon as Dad would open it up, I'd jump right in knowing all along that we'd probably be going somewhere to play some ball. Further, I knew I'd be getting some tasty treats along the way as well. All in all, not a bad deal for me, although Pippin and my two sisters were perhaps a touch jealous about all of these goings on. Now more than ever, each time Dad and I would get into the truck, vociferous howls of despair and injustice would reverberate from inside the house.

Only one of our trips was different. On that day we did not go to the dog park, but instead arrived at the vet's office. I could tell because I could sense and smell the many animals who had come across that threshold, some nervous and afraid, others full of joy. Me, I was full of joy and anticipation. I always liked going to see the vet, because I knew somewhere along the line I'd get a treat or two from somebody there. So in I pranced and received many smiles with admiring remarks from the staff up at the front desk. I was ready for all of the usual routine with the vet followed by the rewards I would receive for my patience. Little did I know at the time that this visit was not going to be routine at all.

I was up on that cold exam table when the vet came in and did the usual poking and prodding, all the time making comments on how handsome I was – I hear that a lot. Then he said to me, "Are you ready for your microchip and rabies shot?" I just looked at him happily, expecting my treat of course. Then Dad came over to hold me tightly. Before I could react that insidious vet reached over with what seemed to me a huge needle and harpooned me in the right shoulder. Ouch!

I let out a pretty loud squeal and struggled with Dad to no avail – boy, did that hurt! I sure was glad my brother and sisters were not around to have heard me let out that squeal though. How embarrassing. I would have been ribbed about it for days. I was just getting over that assault when the dodgy doctor skewered me with a smaller needle. Thankfully, that one didn't hurt nearly as much, and I didn't embarrass myself with an outcry. After that I kept an eye on the crafty devil to see if he was going to inflict anything else on me. Turned out that was it, though, and he gave me a nice tasty biscuit. All was instantly forgiven, but I sure would remember to watch out for any shenanigans from him on my next visit.

Alex wasn't done with trying new things on me during those days. One day he came home with a small black basket looking thing that he called a muzzle. He told me that this was something I would need while riding the public transit in Vienna. Then he proceeded to put this devilish device on me, which I did not appreciate at all. I shook my head and pawed at the detestable thing, but it held fast. Well, I was not going to make a big scene about it, especially since my brother Pippin was watching with a smirk, so I just sat down and looked up at the Chief with a mournful look. Dad checked it and so did Mom for what they called a good fit, then off the torture implement came. As the Chief put the damnable object away, he said, "You'll just have to wear it once in a while, Dude." I looked over at Pippin and gave him a very low growl which wiped that smile off his pointy little face.

CHAPTER 4

November came, and that was when Dad started weighing me all the time. He'd pick me up and settle me on the scale, sometimes placing me in the bag to weigh us both. Every time this occurred he would sit back and shake his head. Finally he and Mom said to me, "Looks like you're over the weight limit for an in-cabin ride, Dude. You'll have to go in the plane's hold in your crate." I wasn't quite sure of what they were talking about, but it didn't sound too good to me. I hoped they weren't thinking of cutting back the old Dude's food intake. That would not go down well with me at all.

It seemed that the Chief had given up on the black bag idea because he stopped bringing it out after a while. He also stopped putting me on that scale, which was fine by me. For a little bit it appeared that things were getting back to a more normal state of affairs around the house. I did miss all of the treats when I was doing the bag trick though.

Alex now spent time tinkering with my crate, putting in some bolts and then attaching a dish to the inside of its front door. Cool, I was getting a custom dish attached to my crate, which was something Pippin would be envious about. I did think it could be a little bit larger to hold more food.

It got well into December, and now it seemed to me that Mom and Dad were talking about Vienna almost all the time.

Both of them had a great deal of eagerness that I could pick up coming off them in waves. It started to make me feel quite excited myself, kind of like when I catch the aroma of bacon cooking in the morning. This feeling that emanated from them continued to grow like a great big ball that was about to pop.

Then one morning when everybody had eaten their breakfast Anne and Alex brought out their suitcases and started packing. I saw that they also were packing some of my things in a little bag. My sisters gave a big look of dismay when they saw this. Pippin came over and sniffed me in query as if to say, 'What gives Dude?' In answer I turned and presented my rear end to him in dismissal. He stalked off with a little growl of envy.

Later in the day Alex took all of us out back and we played an early game of ball until I was a bit on the exhausted side. I wondered if we would have another game at the usual hour. That would be quite a nice bonus for the old Dude. I came back inside and saw that all of the suitcases and my crate were all stacked up by the front door. Now this was December and it was too cold for camping. The only other time I remembered suitcases by the door was when Mom would sometimes go away on a trip for a week or so. Boy I sure hoped that was not going to happen because I always missed Anne so much when she left. I couldn't figure out why my crate was out there too. What was going on?

CHAPTER 5

In the afternoon, Grandma came over all smiles and exuding a whole bunch of anticipation and a bit of nervousness as well. Dad started carting out the suitcases to Grandma's car and then came back and retrieved my crate. It sure looked like somebody was going somewhere. It didn't take me long to find out, because, much to my sibling's consternation, Alex and Anne called me to come with them. With a quick smug smile at Pippin I trotted out the front door and over to Grandma's car. I hopped in eagerly ready to go. Maybe we were all going to the dog park. As we drove off down the street, the howls of injustice and anguish gradually faded away behind us.

After we had driven for a little while, I figured we were not headed to the dog park. We weren't going in the right direction for that. So I really wasn't sure where we were headed, but I could sure sense a great volume of excitement and anticipation in that car. Everybody was chattering on and on like a bunch of crazy squirrels. I thought we must be going to a really cool place indeed!

We finally pulled into a great big parking lot where we all got out. Everybody grabbed bags and Alex had my crate as well. I trotted merrily along on my leash and wondered what new place we were going to. I could smell in the air that snow would be coming soon. We finally reached some automatic doors which, as always, opened before me like magic. I knew about these kind of doors because they are like the ones at the local pet store. 'Welcome Dude,' those doors seemed to say when they whooshed open for me.

Once inside, we got on an elevator, the Dude also knows elevators, because the Dude gets around a lot. The doors swished closed and I could feel that gentle upward movement that meant we would soon arrive at a new place. When those elevator doors opened it was a complete surprise to me – this was no pet supply store, that was for sure.

What unfolded before me was a scene of utter chaos, people were hurrying to and fro everywhere. When I say people, I mean a whole lot of people, more than I had ever seen at one time before. The building was really big to boot, with lots of lights, loud announcements coming out of the air, and many people pushing carts loaded with bags. It was pretty overwhelming at first, but as usual I quickly adjusted and pranced along with my ears bouncing. I heard a whole lot of admiring comments as we made our way into the building. The Dude was on the scene and generating smiles!

Then we came upon something very strange indeed that made me hesitate – moving stairways going upwards and downwards. We were heading straight for the heaving metal, and I have to say that I was more than a little unnerved at walking onto such a thing. Before I had time to worry too much, Alex scooped me up and carried me onto the rolling steel stairway, which he called an escalator. We hopped off at the top, Alex put me back down, and onward we went. Finally we stopped and had to wait around in a line for a while. I sat there and just watched as people went striding by, some with bags, some with large groups of people. They all seemed to me to be in a great big hurry, that was for sure. At one point, a group of ladies all in some sort of uniform stopped and looked at me exclaiming something in words I did not understand at all. I could sense that they were saying admiring things about yours truly, no surprise there.

Eventually we got up to the head of the line and were all called over to a counter by a lady, who lit up with a great big smile when she spotted me. I was having a great time basking in all of the adoration I was getting in this place, no doubt about it. Alex and Anne gave her lots of papers and a couple of what looked like small booklets. They also gave her most of their bags and my crate. She looked all the papers over and asked them some questions while favoring me with more smiles. After a bit she gave them back their booklets along with some other papers and waved goodbye to me. I wished I could have hung around some more to flirt with her.

We went back through the crowds, got into another elevator and went back down. I was surprised to see after we got off that we were back in the big garage again. I thought disappointedly that maybe we were going to go back to the car and then home. It was fun in that big building and I had not had nearly enough time to investigate or to get enough admiration.

Instead of going back to the car, though, we walked over to a little area outside the garage. It turned out to be the smallest dog park I had ever been to before. There wasn't even room enough for the Dude to have a decent game of ball. Anyway, the Chief and Mom kept urging me to get busy, so to keep them happy I complied after having a bit of a sniff around.

When we left the little dog park Mom and Dad turned to Grandma and thanked her for the ride. Grandma gave them both hugs and then came over and hugged me as well. As she walked away from us, I wondered why she was leaving us here in this big parking lot.

As we walked back to the elevator I heard the Chief saying to Mom that the lady at the counter thought I was going to fly in the cabin and not go in the hold. He said that the lady would not have batted an eye if he had shown up with my black bag contraption. The Chief said that next time we all fly, I will be traveling in my black bag instead of a crate. I liked the sound of that because it meant more treats for me for doing the bag thing.

The elevator rose back up and the doors opened on the big fun room again. That made me very pleased because I knew I could spread some more happiness in that place with my grin and bouncing trot.

I turned my head from side to side as we went along. The smiles were in abundance as people regarded me. I liked this place a lot. I thought that Pippin would be totally dazzled if he could sniff all of the new and exotic scents I had picked up in my fur thus far. He would have gone out of his tiny mind if he was here though: too much sensory input for the little numbskull.

We came back to the ticket counter, and Alex spoke to the lady briefly. She smiled at me again and gestured us over to a man who had my crate on a cart. Of course, this man smiled at me too. I was getting light-headed over all of this. We followed him as he wheeled my crate to a little office where there was a man and woman in special uniforms. I don't need to say it...more smiles and you know what. The man in the office opened up my crate and took everything out of it. I was a bit surprised by this. Why would he want my stuff? He looked over everything, nodded, and put it all back inside including my big red chew toy.

Dad picked me up, removed my leash, and gave me a great big hug before passing me to Mom who did the same thing. I could feel a huge rush of feelings from them that contained worry and concern. But one thing that kept me happy and would continue to do so in the upcoming events was the overarching feeling of absolute love that radiated from them both towards me. It felt like basking in warm sunshine while sprawled on cool grass on a fine spring day. I gave both of them vigorous licks and kisses. I knew this would please and reassure them that all was okay. The Dude loves his parents and isn't ashamed to show it!

Mom gave me a final kiss and placed me inside my crate. I didn't like that much as I was rather enjoying all of the attention and pets I was getting from everyone. The man in uniform tied something to my front door, saying something about keeping the door secure. I could see Alex and Anne waving to me as the cart started rolling. The thing was that the cart and I began going away from Mom and Dad who started walking in a different direction. Where were they going without me? Where was I going without them? This was indeed distressing!

We went rolling along through a succession of doors where I finally was unloaded onto one of many larger carts that were attached to what appeared to be a small truck. People went hurrying by, sometimes pausing to look in at me. All around me suitcases of all sizes and shapes were being loaded onto these carts. I wasn't sure what was going on and I sure hoped Anne and Alex would show up soon to bail me out of here. I had never been away from them like this before. Sure there were the times when they left the house for a while, but they always would come back. I could feel a little whine escape from me, everything was so strange. Eventually I laid down and had a nice chew on my toy.

I was jolted out of my reverie by a sudden lurch – we were on the move! Maybe I was being taken home I thought to myself. In a few moments I could feel and see we had come outside. It was cold and lots of snow was coming down, I could see the big building that had been fun earlier silhouetted in a kind of aura of white light. People were looking out of the windows. Boy, I wanted to get back inside there. Very shortly we came to a stop beside something very strange. It looked kind of like a huge steel bird standing out in the snow with its wings fully spread – I sure hoped it wasn't hungry. I could see people loading all of the bags from the truck onto a moving surface that went up inside the big bird's belly. Were they feeding the bags to it in some sinister manner? In a few moments somebody picked up my crate and placed it on this surface – up I went, to what fate I shuddered to imagine.

Instead of being devoured when I got to the top, I was picked up by someone and taken to an area away from most of the bags. Maybe I was being saved for the bird's dessert? Some nice person looked in on me and poured some water into my bowl. I could feel my crate being secured to the floor. Soon everyone in the bird's belly went back down, and I could sense a big door closing. I could feel a vibration throughout this place, a very deep sound similar to what I felt while riding in dad's truck, except a lot more powerful. After a while, we began to move and that vibration became even more intense. I forgot all about being eaten right then. I would have cried and whined, but there was no one around to hear the old Dude so I had another bout of chewing to hopefully help me relax.

We kept rolling along for a period of time and then stopping. At one point we came to a halt and I could feel that vibration build and build until it became a gigantic roar. Suddenly we sprang forward, it felt as though an invisible hand was gently pushing me to the back of the crate. I felt us building up an immense amount of velocity, like when dad speeded up to get on the freeway except maybe a thousand times more intense. Just when I thought things couldn't get any worse, I felt us lift up and up. The steel bird was flying away with me! It felt like I was in the world's biggest elevator that showed no signs of stopping. What would things look like when those doors finally opened?

Finally we stopped climbing, and the roaring vibration settled down into more of a loud hum. I have to say I was darn nervous there for a while. I still didn't like it too much, but I was slowly adapting to this new experience. I sure missed Mom and Dad, though, and wished they would come and let me out. I laid down and began to chew on my toy for a bit. It had been quite a day so far.

I began to doze a bit, but then suddenly perked up. I could sense that Anne and Alex were somewhere on this big bird! I felt both of them and their worry for me. That made me feel a lot better. Even though I wasn't with them, I knew they were near and thinking about me. I relaxed a bit then and for some reason began to ponder how I came to be with them in the first place. It had all really begun with my predecessor, Chester.

CHAPTER 6

When I was but a pup Anne and Alex told me the tale of Chester the rat terrier and his life with them. It is a story I know very well indeed.

Mom and Dad found Chester in a pet store when they still lived in Oregon. They both fell for the feisty little guy in an instant and so home he happily went with them. From his pup-hood he had always struggled with some social issues regarding other dogs, small children, and strangers. Mom worked very hard to cure him of these problems, but he never really got over them. In spite of everything, they still loved him very much, and I am sure he felt the same for them.

Dad used to take Chester – who had grown up to be quite a bit larger than the usual rat terrier – alongside his bicycle for runs along the Willamette River. Chester loved to race along the bike path with Dad very much. Sometimes they would stop next to some of the blackberry bushes that grew close to the path and Chester would delicately nibble some of the choicer berries. Both of them looked forward to this daily routine of bonding with each other.

Chester really enjoyed helping Mom out in her garden as her fearless snail eradicator. When the garden would get beset by the insatiable mollusks, Mom would ask him to hunt them out for her. With great care, Chester would prowl amongst the vegetables and deliver a quick crunching bite to any of the slimy intruders he found.

Anne and Alex also took him camping up in the Cascades at their favorite spot called Frissell Crossing. Chester loved running and charging through the ferns and greenery that made up the lush undergrowth of the forest there. From hearing Mom and Dad talk about this place, it sounded magical to me, as it must have been for Chester. I want to go and visit this place someday with all my siblings.

When Chester was just six years old, his vet found out he had a bad thing called lymphoma. I don't know what that is, but from the telling, Mom and Dad were absolutely devastated. Chester was so young and vibrant still, it was hard for them to fathom this news. They decided to try a treatment called chemotherapy in hopes that Chester might get better. Dad said Chester was a very brave boy to endure these treatments, because they made him very sick. When he came home after these regimens sometimes he would soil himself, and wearily he would make his way to the bathtub for Mom or Dad to clean him. He felt better and more himself after a bath and equated the bathtub with getting well.

While Chester was mid-way through the treatments, Mom and Dad moved from Oregon to Colorado where he continued the chemo stuff. When all of the treatments finally came to an end, Chester seemed to be back to his old self. I'll bet he was glad not to have to return to the vet's office, because it was something he probably connected with sickness and pain.

During this time Alex and Anne had rented a place in the mountains, which Chester, who now was feeling really great, enjoyed ever so much. The daily excursions out into the aspen and pine lined trails made him soar with happiness. He loved to race across the meadows and charge through the forest exploring all kinds of new sniffs. It seemed everything was going to be all right.

Sadly, about a year after the end of his chemo the lymphoma came back. One week he was streaking with glee through the aspen groves enjoying the hike they were all on, and then within a short span of time he had faltered rapidly. Soon the fearless charger of the trails and bike paths was reduced to a hobbling premature old man. Poor Chester could hardly negotiate the stairs to the house now. He could no longer jump up on the bed to sleep with Mom and Dad. Sometimes they would find him downstairs in the bathroom waiting for one of them to give him a healing bath. Unfortunately the baths no longer worked as they had in the past. He finally kind of separated from Mom and Dad by staying to himself, as if he was getting them both used to the idea he would be going soon.

Then one day they found that Chester could not even go down the stairs outside to relieve himself. Alex had to carry the poor guy down. Dad told me that after they got down the stairs, Chester looked up at him with eyes that said clearly, "This is it my friend, we've had a great run together, but it's time to go. Help me move onward now." Later that day Pete the vet came to the house, and with Mom and Dad by Chester's side, his spirit was released to once more race through the aspen groves with reckless abandon.

Mom and Dad were grief stricken over the loss of their

beloved rat terrier. At first they told each other that never again would they get a dog and form such a deep attachment to it. They believed the sorrow and pain of another possible loss was just too much to bear. I think they both unconsciously knew that a hole remained where Chester had been, and they would need to eventually fill it.

After about a month had passed, Anne began talking about how cute Jack Russells were and how they were so like a smaller version of Chester. Dad got interested as well and before long the interest turned to research and finally to actually considering a new addition to the family. Many websites of local breeders were looked at, as well as local ads in various papers, but no Jack puppies seemed to be available at that time.

Then one evening in September Anne found a breeder's website that had just posted pictures of a new batch of Jack Russell puppies, including yours truly. Both Mom and Dad were very excited, but still not really sure if they wanted to take a little one back into their lives. In the end, they decided there was no harm to go and have a look, so they made an appointment with the breeder to visit. Here is where I came onto the scene.

Mom and Dad had one guy that they had in mind from the website pictures, one of my brothers. When they arrived at the breeder's house all six of us pups were introduced to them. This was my first sight of Anne and Alex. My little nub of a tail vibrated profusely when each of them petted and held me. I couldn't get enough of them and kept going from one to the other. These people felt right to me! I could tell that my sister Daisy felt that way too; she could not get enough either. After what seemed to me too short of a time, they got up and said goodbye to us all. My heart sank. Where were they going?

In the weeks that followed other people came to visit, but I did not feel drawn to any of them as I had to Anne and Alex. One day a couple came and left with my sister Daisy, which made me very sad. One thing that was peculiar, though, was that Susie, my owner lady, kept telling the other people who came that I was reserved. Reserved for what? I was too young to understand all of this.

On Halloween evening I was fast asleep, cuddled with my brothers and sisters. I had a very strange dream in which I was alone in the dead of night in an aspen forest. There was a full moon overhead that illuminated the aspen's white bark eerily. I felt terribly afraid – after all, I was just a little guy. Where were my mother and siblings?

Suddenly a dog quietly trotted out of the forest and came to an abrupt halt in before me. I gathered my courage and asked who he was and where was this place. He said, "This place and my name are of no importance." He stared at me for a moment and then continued, "I have a message to impart to you, little one. Very soon you will be leaving your home to begin a new life. I want you to know that you will be going to a very loving home with two people who already adore you." He continued, "It is your duty to be a worthy dog and look after them. You must be well-mannered and friendly to all people and – hard as it is – to other dogs as well. I can only ask that you try as best you can to get along with cats." He stopped then and regarded me with brown eyes that seemed full of tears. Finally he said, "I loved them with all of my heart. I hope they knew that." Then he turned and slowly walked away, disappearing into the dark of the forest. From out of the gloom his voice came once more, "Take good care of them, little one."

I was awakened abruptly from my dream and brought out into the living room. To my great surprise Alex and Anne were standing there with big smiles waiting for me. I can tell you my little tail was vibrating a mile a minute. This time, when they left I went with them to embark on my new life. When we arrived home in the dark, I could see that we were surrounded by aspen trees gently soughing in the night breeze. It seemed I heard a voice floating on the air saying, "Remember, take good care of them."

CHAPTER 7

The big bird suddenly got a lot louder again and startled me awake. I had drifted off to sleep for I don't know how long. I felt us gently going down and began to get excited. What would be revealed to me when those doors opened? I hoped it would be Mom and the Chief waiting to greet me. I could still sense them on the bird, which was reassuring.

Then came a couple of big bounces followed by a huge roar from the bird's wings. Again I felt that invisible hand push at me as we decelerated rapidly. As we slowed to a pace that was similar to driving in the chief's truck, I could sense we were back on land again. Finally we stopped and the doors opened, letting in a rush of fresh moist air. My heart soared; I had survived the belly of the big bird. The Dude was on solid ground again!

People came in and unstrapped my crate while looking in and, of course smiling when they saw me. The funny thing was that when they talked to me, it was in words I had never heard before. I could tell that I was being admired though. I was put back onto that moving table and eventually onto another strange truck. Again people were hurrying to unload all the cases and baggage. I sat in my crate looking around for any sign of Alex and Anne. When I looked up at a big building with lots of windows, I saw lots of people looking out, but they were too small for me to make out. Still, I could sense Mom and Dad were somewhere near and now feeling somewhat relieved.

The truck jolted forward, and we were off again. There was a light rain coming down, but the morning sun broke through a layer of clouds overhead. It made me feel better to see the sun again. We stopped, and someone came over to refill my now empty water dish. Then I was put on another truck, which whisked me away to arrive at the feet of yet another big steel bird. This bird, though large, was not nearly the stature of the one from which I had just been released. Sure enough my crate was soon lifted into this bird's belly. When would this ordeal be over?

Well, at least I knew what to expect this time; the acceleration, the climbing, and leveling off. It was still scary, but not nearly as much as the first time. With my keen senses, I knew that Mom and Dad were on this bird as well, and that was a comfort. I wondered how my brother and sisters were doing back home. Were they still howling in indignation and injustice? I knew they would really be howling in fear now if they had the adventures I had experienced up to this point. They are all a good pack of Jacks but so much more high strung than the Dude.

After a short time I felt the bird start to descend again. 'That was quick,' I thought to myself. Soon came the bumps and jolts, the roar of deceleration, and finally we stopped moving. The doors cranked open and in came the people to unload me with the baggage. Once again I was put on a truck after being admired by more than a few people. Where would

I be taken to now? I noticed that it was late afternoon now; the sun was getting low in the clear sky.

Instead of being taken to another steel bird, I was transported inside a building and unloaded onto a cart. A woman came and beamed a big smile when she looked in at me. She began pushing the cart forward and through a pair of large doors, finally stopping and placing my crate on a low table. With a wave she left me and trundled away with the cart. I looked out into a big room with lots of people carrying or wheeling bags. There were also very peculiar roundish looking contraptions with bags going round and round on them. Some of these things were still and empty for a bit but then would suddenly erupt into life with flashing lights and a loud buzzing sound. Very soon after this display, bags would belch forth, then people would gather and pluck them randomly off as they attempted to make their circular journey.

I began to feel like my poor bladder was going to explode soon. After all, more than a few hours had passed since the old Dude had been outside to do his business. Suddenly I spotted Anne and the Chief hurrying towards me from across the room. All thoughts of doing some business instantly went away as Alex opened the door of my crate, attached my leash, and finally sprung me from the crate. Hooray! I was back with Mom and Dad! My tail was vibrating so fast that I felt I was flying.

CHAPTER 8

After many, many licks, hitch-walks, and happy butt wiggling, I was more than ready to go wherever Alex and Anne wanted. I was back with them now and that was all that mattered. They picked up their bags from the moving machine and loaded them onto a cart along with my crate. I pranced along very happily as we proceeded out of the big room down a long corridor. Along the way, many people were giving me the look and smiling. We went through some doors and walked up to a strange man holding a sign. After speaking to Dad for a moment, he beckoned us all to follow him through another set of doors that opened to a parking lot. Dad and the man took our cart over to a van where they began loading everything in. Mom tried coaxing me to do some business, but I was too darned excited to even think about that.

Unfortunately for me, I was put back into the crate by the Chief. I sure did not appreciate that at all and let him and Anne know about it as we drove out of the lot. At least both of them could reach in and give me some finger pets though; that made it somewhat more bearable. Anne even handed in some pieces of bread that I could munch. I was pretty hungry, no doubt about it, but still too excited to really think about it much. I could hardly wait for this ride to get over, because I wanted to be out of this crate and start investigating where we were.

I sniffed the air as we drove, but nothing was remotely familiar to me. Soon I could tell we were in a city of some sort from the stopping and starting of the van, various honking of horns, and the overall smell. Were we in Denver? I didn't think so; it did not feel the way Denver did. Finally the van rolled to a stop, and the doors clicked open. After everything was unloaded, I was once again freed from what I had started to consider my little prison. I looked around and saw a lot of very tall and old buildings around me. Where were we?

Right away, Dad turned and disappeared inside a building next to where we were dropped off. Mom once again tried to get me to do my thing in a patch of bushes, but I was too busy marveling at my surroundings. There were going to be so many new and interesting sniffs to be had around here, I was sure of that.

The Chief came out of the building with an older woman who gave me a glowing smile of...well, you know. Ha, even after a long, tiring journey, I still looked good. She beckoned us to follow her and so with all of our bags and crate in tow we trailed her around to the side of the structure. We passed through an iron gate that led into a courtyard then went through a doorway into a large foyer. Mom, the lady, and I got into a very small elevator that rose up a few floors, stopped and opened onto a small hallway. We got off, and proceeded a short ways down the hall and came to another door, which the lady opened for us. The door opened into what was the inside of a small house complete with an entranceway that had hangers for coats, hats and leashes. Quickly I trotted in to investigate. The entranceway led into a small kitchen and then into one larger room that had tables, chairs, and a bed. It was a really nice little place and, best of all, there were no other dogs! One thing that puzzled me, though, was that there was no doggy door for me. I wasn't too worried though; I knew the Chief would figure something out.

Dad caught up with us soon and after setting everything in the living room, began talking with Mom and the lady. About that time, I remembered that my bladder was about to burst and tried desperately to get their attention. I tried pawing at Dad and then Mom, but alas to no avail – they were both too preoccupied in conversation. Well, I hate to say it, but the Dude just let go and released the floodgates right there on the kitchen floor. That got everyone's attention quickly, I'll tell you. I looked up and smiled at them all with relief. Boy, did that ever feel good!

There was a moment of startled silence and then a lot of talk, followed by the lady laughing and shaking her head. I could see the Chief and Mom relax after that. Mom hurried to get my large pond cleaned up, with a little bit of admonishment directed at me. I took it with my usual coolness and gave her some extra kisses to say that the Dude was sorry.

Soon the lady gave the Chief some keys and, with a wink at me, went out the front door. After she left, Dad turned to me and said, "Welcome to Vienna, boy!" We had arrived at the mystical place at long last. Now maybe I would find out what all the fuss was about.

The Chief said the name of our new home in Vienna was Apartments Augarten and it was owned by someone named Beatrix. He said the apartments were in a great location and had what he called a U-Bahn station right in front of them, so it would be easy to get around in Vienna. He also said there was a restaurant owned by Beatrix's family on the ground floor of our building that we should try. I didn't really fathom all of what he said, but I was sure I would find out in time.

A little later there was a knock on the door, and of course I hastened to be the first to greet whoever was there. Mom opened the door and found that it was our landlady, Beatrix, who smiled down at me sunnily. I immediately came out with an exaggerated display of hitch-walk as she entered the room. I sure wanted to make a better impression with her than I had with the previous lady, and hitch-walk is way better than ponds on the floor any day!

Beatrix reached down and gave me a scratch in just the right place behind my ears – I liked Beatrix a lot! She talked with Mom and Dad for a bit, asking if they had any questions about the apartment or the neighborhood. After a bit she bade us all goodbye and favored me with another warm smile as she went out the door.

After Beatrix left, we all decided to go out and reconnoiter the neighborhood. I trotted along happily and took in all of the new scents in this unfamiliar place. There were long blocks of nice old buildings, and I could sense that there were many people living in them. I was guessing that in Vienna many people lived in small houses like the one we had.

Eventually we stopped in front of a well-lit building with large windows. I could see a lot of people inside this place pushing carts around. Dad said this place was called Billa and he was going in to shop. Being the Dude and with my super sense of smell, I could tell it was a food store of some sort. Anyway in he went while Mom and I remained outside, much to my disappointment. Pretty soon Dad reappeared, smiling and bearing a few loaded shopping bags.

We strolled back to our apartment and Mom unloaded the contents of the bags. Much to my delight, Mom opened up a can of something that smelled delicious. My stomach rumbled and reminded me of how long it had been since I had eaten a good meal. Anne put the wonderful smelling concoction into my bowl and set it down before me. I made short work of that, I'll tell you; it was great wet food, nothing like the dry kibble we usually get at home. I was going to like this trip now, I could tell.

After my gourmet meal was gobbled up, I took Mom and Dad for another stroll in our new neighborhood. The city smells were numerous and so varied. I could tell there were a great number of dogs that walked in this area and wondered what Vienna dogs would be like. It was pretty darned cold as well, so, as quickly as I could, I found a bit of grass and took care of a great deal of business. Dad had some special bags for cleanup after I was done. He said that in a city like Vienna it was the proper thing to do and that not to do so could result in a big fine as well. I sure was glad that Mom and Dad knew all of these things, because I wouldn't want them to get in trouble with anybody.

We walked back towards our new home, but instead of going up to our apartment, we went to the front door of our building which Dad had gone into when we had arrived. I could now smell wondrous things wafting from behind that door. This was a restaurant!

In many walks back home, I had passed by some of these establishments and could sniff many delicious things coming from their environs. I was never allowed to go inside of one of these delectable-smelling establishments in Colorado; the Dude either had to wait in the car or at home while Anne and Alex went to a restaurant. I never liked that, because the Dude should go everywhere and be welcomed by all, especially in places that had wonderful-smelling food! Mom had often remarked that the rules for dogs going to restaurants in the USA were ridiculous and backward. Ahh, Mom, I love the way she thinks. I believe she is a big Jack Russell too, just like Dad.

So anyway, there we were in front of this restaurant, and I thought we would just continue on by after pausing. I was quite surprised when Dad opened the door for Mom and gave a little tug on my leash telling me to come along too. Quickly I recovered from my astonishment and trotted inside. I was ready to investigate my first restaurant and the heavenly scents that came from within.

The place was very crowded with what Dad said were Christmas revelers having what looked and smelled like very fine meals. I sure would have liked to try some bites of those dishes! The whole place contained a jolly type of atmosphere and warmth, which rolled over me like a soothing wave. It was a feeling similar to Christmastime at home. I liked this place a lot!

A lady greeted us as we came in and began to lead us to an empty table surrounded by all the merrymakers. I heard many comments directed at me as we made our way there, but I couldn't understand the words they were saying. Be that as it may, the Dude can tell when someone is giving him the compliments, no matter what the language. Mom signaled for me to lay down under the table, and I readily complied. This was a great new experience! The lady went away but soon returned with a bowl of water just for me. I thought that if Pippin could see me now his muzzle whiskers would curl with envy.

Mom and Dad proceeded to have their meal, which smelled divine to my little nose. They both gave me little bites under the table, which I accepted with barely restrained eagerness. Many people who came in later would notice me and…you know the drill by now. Much as I wanted to get up and go visit all of the admiring folks around me, I kept myself under that table. I wanted Mom and the Chief to remember how good I was so they would take me along to many more of these places.

After our meal, we had another short stroll so I could take care of some things. When I had concluded my duties, we walked back to our new home and prepared for bed. I did a little of what Mom calls "wild dog," which is me joyfully and fiercely romping in the bed covers. Eventually I settled into the warm spot between Mom and Dad and slipped into a nice deep sleep. It had been a long journey, but I had made it – best of all I was the only dog, with no siblings to contend with. Life was good!

CHAPTER 9

That night as I drifted off I thought about my true sister, Daisy, and how we came to be separated and then re-united. It is a story I love to tell.

Daisy was one of the first of my real siblings to go away with a new human family. It was very sad for me as a pup because she and I had been great playmates, loving to rough-house together as pups do. She and I slept cuddled together with all the rest of the little ones. I knew she was fond of me because she would sometimes try to protect me from the other pups who tried to get fierce with me. Even as a little one Daisy could be very ferocious; most of the brood feared and respected her.

We were all together playing one day when a man and woman came to visit us. The people seemed nice but, as I have said before, did not have the same pull on me that Mom and Dad did. They picked up Daisy and petted her, finally nodding to each other and our owner lady.

We all went back to playing and cavorting around while the people sat down at a table and did something with a lot of papers. They finally got up smiling, and the woman came over to pick up my sister. This time she did not put her back down, though; she and the man walked out the front door. My last glimpse of Daisy was of her looking out at me from the cradle of the woman's arms with a very worried expression on her face.

In the following weeks, one of my brothers and another sister went out of my life. Sometimes I would wake up in the morning and someone would be missing. Other times it would happen in the same way as Daisy leaving. It seemed we were all being plucked away, never to see or play with each other again. It was all a little depressing to a little guy. What was happening to my family?

Well, as I described before, my turn came, and away I went with Mom and Dad. Time passed, and I kind of forgot about all of my former family. My new family consisted now of Mom and Dad plus an older dog named William. There were also two squirrel-looking things called cats. I won't tell all of their stories now, maybe some other time in the future. I will tell you that from my experiences cats are not my favorite animals. Don't tell Mom or the Chief, though.

About a year had gone by, during which we had moved down from the mountains to our new home in Longmont, Colorado. Our new house had a great big back yard that was just made for me and the ball. Anne and Alex began talking about getting a playmate that was more around my size and age. William was too old and grumpy, he did not like to play with a precocious little dude like me. We won't talk about those darned cats. Suffice to say I had a lot of energy and needed a friend.

One day Mom and the Chief took me in the car for a drive. I was not sure where we were going, but that was okay because I got to go! We drove for what seemed to me at the time to be an eternity. One thing was for sure; the smells I was getting were pretty unfamiliar so I knew we were going somewhere I had not been to before.

We finally arrived at our destination and the sniffs I was getting there stirred something in me. At first I was unsure what this was, but once I got out of the car it hit me. I was back at my original home!

I wondered if we had come to visit my mother and any siblings that remained. My nub of a tail vibrated at the thought of that. It would be nice to see my mother again. We were met at the door by my original owner lady, Susie, who smiled brightly at me and, of course, had all kinds of nice things to say about me. We all went inside of the house and then out into the backyard where I got a big surprise. Out there sniffing along the fence line was another Jack Russell who looked vaguely familiar.

We approached each other a little warily, circled and then did a huge amount of sniffing to make sure of things. We paused, memories came flooding back, then tails began to vibrate and wag in recognition – it was my sister Daisy. She pranced around me in total joy and happiness. I felt so happy I lost some of my usual reserve and began to chase her around the yard with glee.

As we cavorted, I could feel Mom and Dad's apparent relief, as if some barrier had been overcome or removed. When we had stopped our game of chase for a breather, Daisy went over to Mom and gave her a thorough licking, much to Mom's delight of course. Mom does love her Jack kisses, no doubt about that. After she was done greeting Mom, Daisy ran over to the Chief and proceeded to give him some very wet kisses as well.

Mom and Dad looked at each other and started back to the house. I sensed that we would be leaving soon, and it made me very sad. I wanted to stay and play with my sister. Dad scooped me up, and we went back into the house towards the front door. It was then I noticed that Mom was following us with Daisy cradled in her arms. Daisy was coming with us?

We all got in our car and away we went with Daisy, who seemed a little nervous and unsure. I was so darn happy and tried to reassure her that all would be well now that we were back together. I wondered also what had happened to her and where she went after I had last seen her.

From hearing Mom and Dad tell it, Daisy was adopted by the two people who took her away with them when we were so young. She had been raised in the big city of Denver in what Dad called a condo. He had said in a rather scoffing tone, "A condo is no place to raise a Jack Russell. No room to run in a condo." I sure didn't know what a condo was, but if there was no room to run then I was sure I would not like it.

Mom had said that Daisy's two people were getting something called a divorce and were going to live apart from each other. She went on to say that as a consequence of this they brought Daisy back to Susie and asked her to find my sister a new home. 'Poor Daisy,' I had thought to myself, 'No wonder she was so nervous and unsure of what was going on when we drove home that day.' In the end, it was perfect timing because Dad, by some quirk of fate, had called Susie the very next day looking for a playmate for me.

We all soon found out that Daisy was kind of a tenderfoot, because the first day we took her out on a trail, she got a sticker in her foot. Rather than shake it off or get it with her teeth, like I always do, she just sat her butt down and refused to walk any further. Silly girl would not move until Mom ministered to her pink little foot with a lot of soothing. Mom and Dad said she had been raised like a little princess in the city and did not know how to deal with unpaved trails. She also had to learn about squirrels, but that she picked up very quickly and now keeps the yard pretty clear of those scurrilous knaves.

I don't know where she got a hatred of crows, but she really does not like those cawing tricksters at all. I really never gave them a thought until she taught me how unholy and unsavory they are. Now, whenever any of those winged devils dare to fly over our yard or, worse yet, have the temerity to alight in one of our trees, they are faced with a chorus of howls and barks, until they finally depart in shame and disgrace. Of course the Dude doesn't rouse himself to do this unless he hears from the length and pitch of the cacophony the brother and sisters put up that his voice is seriously needed to repel the feathered harpy's incursion into his domain.

In the end, Daisy settled in with us as neat as you please. She has tough feet now and takes the trails just like an old pro. Both of us still like to play a good game of tug together with her allowing me to drag her across the rug attached to the other end of our rope toy. We always get along and, like in our pup-hood, she protects me from the younger siblings when they get out of hand. She makes sure that the Dude does not have to get out of his mellow zone to deal with their juvenile problems.

I am very happy we took that drive back then and brought her home. I know Daisy is very happy and content to be here as well and reigns as the high queen over Lily and Pippin. That's the way it is in our pack and also the way I like it.

CHAPTER 10

I woke up pretty early in the morning; in fact it was still quite dark outside. I could tell because I could still see lights shining diffusely through the curtained windows. No matter, the Dude had a full bladder and needed to get outside relatively fast. I jumped down off the bed and began to serenade Mom and Dad with my grunts-and-groans song. I quickly followed this up with an accompaniment of staccato scratching at the front door.

The desired effect was achieved in a very short span of time. I would say I only got about three lines of my virtuoso performance done before the Chief popped out of bed and hastily got dressed. I am sure he did not want a repeat of the pond-making I did the previous day in the kitchen, or worse. For that matter, neither did I – that would be too embarrassing for the Dude. I gave the Chief another reprise of my song, though, just to hurry him along a bit. Dad shrugged into his jacket and placed a hat on his very thinly furred head, and we were off.

It was cold and dark outside as we made our way to an area I was starting to consider my patch of ground. I think that the Chief was perhaps a little miffed the patch I had chosen was three blocks away from our Vienna home. Being the Dude, on the other hand, I liked this stroll; there were plenty of places to stop and sniff along the way, much to the chagrin of the shivering Chief.

With business taken care of, we made our way back to the apartment, with a few sniff stops along the way. The Dude has to read the local papers, you know. The sun was starting to make its way up as we entered the courtyard of our new home, and I felt rumblings in my stomach. I thought a generous breakfast of that nice Viennese dog food would go down quite well.

When we came through the door to our place, it was so nice and warm. Mom was up and had coffee brewing for her and the grateful Chief. I caught a whiff of the cold cuts, bread and jam that Mom was laying out. I sure hoped she wouldn't forget the Dude! My concern was short lived, though, and soon I was gulping up more of that great Austrian dog fare. I would love telling Pippin about this gastronomic treat when I got back home. I could picture him running in circles of disbelief and envy as I related to him in detail the exquisite taste of this cuisine. Life can be so fun sometimes.

After the Chief and Mom finished their breakfast (of course I got some tasty bites off the plates as well), they proceeded to shower and get ready for the day. To hurry them along a bit, I performed a variation of my whimper-and-grunt song. Very soon we were out on the street. My ears were pricked up, and I trotted along excitedly – I was ready to explore Vienna!

We walked over to a building in front of our apartment block and stopped in front of a row of machines. To me they looked similar to what the Chief often used back home to get what he called money out of. Instead of this machine spitting out money, though, it produced some small bits of paper that the Chief called U-Bahn tickets. I was not sure what a U-Bahn was, but I sure hoped it wasn't another big steel bird.

After Dad got the tickets, we walked around the building and went down a staircase that led below the structure. There were many people hurrying to and fro when we got to the bottom of the stairs; some, having seen me, broke in to the usual smiles. I thought Vienna was going to suit me just fine.

Right about then, the Chief put a damper on my merry mood by taking out that darned muzzle and putting it on me. I thought to myself, 'How in the world will any of the Viennese be able to appreciate my handsome face with this ugly black basket covering it?' I didn't cause a ruckus about it though; the Dude maintains his dignity despite the minor humiliations the Chief subjects him to.

We soon came to a set of those escalator stairs, but this time I knew the Chief would be picking me up so I was not worried. We hopped on the rolling metal and went further down. From below I could hear some strange sounds. First came a faint whooshing that built quickly to a rumbling roar. The roar culminated in a squealing sound as if something very large was coming to an abrupt halt. Then there was a brief silence. Shortly, though, a series of loud clicks sounded, followed by sliding noises as if a lot of automatic doors were opening at once. I heard the footsteps of a lot of people then. I wondered if they might be running away from whatever it was that had arrived down there. A voice came out of the air and said something in that language I could not understand. Then once more there was the slide and click and a whistle-like sound, and a gentle rumble began. The rumble soon built to a roar along with some more whooshing. The roar quickly began to fade away, as if whatever caused that noise was speeding away very fast into the distance. I began to get a little nervous about jumping off at the bottom of that escalator.

We came down to a big platform area where – to my great relief – there were many people standing around and waiting. Their calm demeanor, along with Mom and Dad's, reassured me that whatever had caused those noises was not some kind of horrible giant squirrel or crow. So with my usual coolness – despite the basket on my face that seemed to grow larger every minute – I sat down and waited with everybody else.

As I looked around I noticed that on either end of the platform there were big black yawning openings that had dim lighting stretching along as far as I could see. 'Ha!' I thought to myself, 'Those are tunnels.' I remembered tunnels from some of the drives my siblings and I had taken with Mom and Dad in the mountains around Colorado.

We were all out for a family drive in the mountains when all of us Jacks first experienced a tunnel. The blackness suddenly appeared before us encompassing the whole road like a giant open mouth with no teeth. To me it looked as if the thing was poised there waiting to swallow us all up in one big gulp. We had all been a bit nervous as we neared the huge gaping maw; Pippin – the little chicken – had even whimpered a bit. I think I might have ducked a bit as we drove right into the dimly-lit darkness. Thank goodness Pippin or Lily had not seen that! Eventually we had come out the other side into daylight without a scratch on our furry little rear ends. Nope, there was nothing scary about tunnels that I could remember.

I was about to give the Chief a paw on the leg and a sorrowful look – hopefully to get him to remove the now seemingly gigantic apparatus that obscured my muzzle – when I heard a faint rumble. The ominous noise was issuing forth from the tunnel mouth closest to us, and it began to grow. You know, I sure was glad I had heard all of this before. Even if I did not know what was coming, I was in control. The Dude had been in the belly of two big steel birds and survived without so much as a flea bite, so this would be a piece of biscuit.

I could now feel a rush of warm air coming from the tunnel mouth, which felt kind of good as it washed over me. The rumble soon built into a roar, and I spotted some lights zooming out of the darkness of the opening. I was mesmerized: what was this thing? I didn't have to wait long because from out of the blackness came blasting forth what appeared to be small train with lots of cars. What a letdown and sort of a relief that a little train was responsible for all that cacophony. Yeah, the Dude knows trains and they don't scare him, unless of course they blow their horns when I am close by.

The train came whistling in and squealed to a halt. I looked up with a grin at the Chief and Mom who had apparently been watching me to get my reaction to all of this. I think they were pleased to see that the doughty Dude had sat through the whole scene without twitching a whisker.

The doors on all of the train's cars clicked and slid open, then lots of people came out. Being as how I am so smart, I knew what was coming next, so without any urging I led Mom and Dad onto the train, much to their further amazement, I'm sure. After we got inside, Mom and the Chief sat down, the doors slid shut with a loud snap, the voice from out of the air said something, and, with the sound of the whistle, we were off. I must say that the speed built up quick, but it was not anything like those steel birds. I balanced myself and adjusted quickly to the shimmies and shakes the train gave. I felt like I was riding a big skateboard, just like some Jacks I had seen on television, except I did not have to push – the Dude was being conveyed.

It was kind of a fun time on the U-Bahn, the train would get going real fast and then, just as before, squeal to a stop and go through the same routine when it picked us up. People would get off and on, and many gave me what I will call "the look" of admiration and smiles. They did this in spite of that blasted grotesque fixture on my face. I thought that they would most likely melt if they saw me without it. Some of these people would talk with Mom and Dad about me in that strange language, which Dad later told me was German. I could sense that my presence was causing great warming and cheer in their souls, no matter what the language was. I am just universally cute – that's all there is to it!

After a few stops, we finally came to the one Mom and Dad wanted, so up and off we went. I exited the car with my usual prancing trot and my ears at the alert. I really wanted to be rid of the black plastic appendage on my nose. I swear it was growing larger and heavier by the minute. The station we got off at was much bigger and had many more people rushing around. As I looked around, I saw another dog walking his people. I think it was some sort of fluffy poodle from what I could make out. What really interested me was that the dog was also wearing a muzzle. I thought to myself, 'Oh joy! The Dude is not the only one to suffer this ignominy in public!'

We came to the escalator again and, with me cradled this time in Mom's arms, took it going upwards. At the top of the stairs, Mom put me down and – to my immense relief and gratefulness – removed the hated black instrument of torture. Free at last!

I saw we were coming to another set of stairs, this time the non-moving kind, and I led Mom and the Chief upwards towards daylight. Dad remarked that we were now in a place called Stephansplatz, in the center of old Vienna. He and Mom were wondering between themselves if it had changed much since their last visit years ago. I thought that wherever this place was, it had better live up to all the months of hype the Chief had been giving it. After all, it takes more than a few tall buildings and trains to impress the Dude. When we reached the top of the stairs and I looked around, I had to stop short in surprise.

What surrounded me made my eyes feel like they were popping out like that little obnoxious Chihuahua dog in my neighborhood. Stephansplatz was a very large cobblestoned square almost entirely encircled by very tall buildings. The contrast was amazing in those structures; some looked old and grand, while others had the gleam and polish of modern architecture. How do I know about architecture, you might ask? Well, I will leave that for another time. Suffice it to say that when a Jack hangs around Mom and Dad long enough, he tends to pick up knowledge on a myriad of subjects.

There was one building that stood out from all in its sheer magnificence. This one the Chief said was St. Stephansdom Cathedral. I was quite taken by its elegant towering spires and pointed arches. The Chief said it was constructed in the Gothic style of architecture. I thought it looked mighty impressive for something so old. The very steep roof was tiled in what appeared to be a mosaic of colored tiles. One section had a large two-headed bird, which seemed very strange to me. Dad said it was a double eagle, the symbol of Austria from the old Habsburg days. I didn't know who old Habsburg was, but he must have been pretty powerful to have such a gigantic eagle portrayed on the roof of a cathedral.

After taking in all of the buildings and the great cathedral around me, my eyes came back to the square itself. Stephansplatz was full of lots of people going every which way. Many stood in the center of the square and marveled at the building as I did. It was a little drizzly out, but that sure did not stop all of these people from wandering around the great open space. I saw many shops, restaurants, and a few places Mom called cafés or coffee houses. People seemed to flow in and out of all of these establishments in an endless tide. I thought I had seen a lot of people at Denver airport, but that seemed miniscule compared to this place. I found myself in awe of the whole scene.

We began walking across the square and up one of the large cobblestoned streets that connected to it. From my point of view, trotting along as I was, it was all the ankles and shoes of the multitudes of people. It was darn hard to get a clear look upwards at the buildings that continued to rise around us like a canyon. As we progressed up the large street, which the Chief referred to as the Graben, the crowds became a bit thinner, and I could see a bit of what we were passing.

It appeared the Graben was like some great outdoor mall with shops lining both sides of the streets. As in the square, there was a continual flow of people in and out of these establishments. I was not too interested in them, though; there were no delectable smells of tender morsels emanating from any of them that I could discern. As we neared what appeared to be the end of the Graben my nose started picking up a whole plethora of enticing scents. I pinpointed the building: it was dead on at the ending of the street, and we were heading right for it. Excellent!

Much to my dismay we stopped outside and just peered in the very large windows. I could see all kinds of items in those windows that I would have loved to sample, that's for sure! I heard Dad say that this store, called Julius Meinl, probably did not allow dogs. I didn't know who this Julius fellow was, but I wished he would come out to meet me. I believe that he would have melted and begged the Dude's forgiveness, inviting him to enter and partake of all the delicacies he smelled in there.

It was not to be, though. Instead we turned and proceeded down another large street. We walked along, and now the aromas of new and wonderful treats seemed to come at me from everywhere. They got especially strong when we passed a place Dad called Demel. He said this used to be the favorite confection shop for the old Habsburgs. I could understand that by the sweet fragrances that issued forth from the place. This old Habsburg guy must really enjoy it in there.

We passed Demel and continued on through the now increasing crowds. About then I began to perceive some faint sounds, a sort of clip-clopping that was increasing as we walked along. I squinted ahead, but there were too many people in the way, so I could not make out the source of this unsettling noise. Clop-clop, clop-clop! My ears pricked up in worried alertness: clop-clop, clop-clop, echoing off all the buildings along the street, assaulting my senses from every side. I could make out the top of a big arching entranceway that seemed to be blocking the street ahead, but all the darned people obscured my view of the ground. What was making those disconcerting sounds? We got nearer to the end of the street, and the booming, rhythmic sounds now seemed to be like the ticking of an enormous tower clock right next to my little head. What new peril was I going to pass through now?

We burst through the crowd suddenly, and I saw the source of my discomfort. Clopping and clacking around a square and through the great entranceway in the building were pairs of horses that were pulling small carriages. Seen from my vantage point, those horses were enormous. They had lots of leather over and around them, including some pieces that nearly covered their eyes. Some of the mammoth things were even festooned with what looked like big bird feathers. Immediately I tried to beat a hasty retreat back down the street.

All the horses I had ever seen before were from a distance or on the television at home, where a Jack could growl and bark at them from the safety of the couch. It made a huge difference to see them up close and in person! I'll tell you something else: the Dude wasn't about to bark at any horse with plumage! Well, at least not while they were clopping around so close to me anyway. I think what frightened me the most, though, was the sound of their feet reverberating so very loudly off of all of the buildings. That and the fact that they had their vision obscured by the leather pieces. Blind horses? I could get stepped on by those big nasty hooves! I could almost imagine Pippin's mirth at being told that The Dude had been squashed by a leather-bound creature decorated with feathers. I thought that going back to Demel's or Julius Meinl would be a great idea right about then.

Dad and Mom looked down at me to see why I was pulling back the way we had come. I could see that they both realized the source of my unease right away, because they began making soothing noises at me. I still was not happy despite their efforts, but at least we did not go any closer to those huge beasts, and they did not seem to be blindly blundering over towards me.

With great reluctance on my part and much tugging on my leash by the Chief, we walked through a side passage by the entranceway. The noisome clopping echoed even louder than before in that enclosed space, so I began pulling the Chief along to get out of there quicker. Thankfully we got to the other side of the passage unscathed. As we exited, I saw a nice park-like area that was next to the street. To my great relief, we left the cobblestones and walked out onto the grass, leaving that horrid sound of the horse tramping behind. Soon I was back to my usual Dude-like composure.

Out on the safety of the grass, I investigated one of the

carriages from a distance as it clacked and clopped down the street. I could see that there was a person who sat on a bench behind the horses holding some long lines with which he seemed to guide the enormous creatures – he was their driver! Seated behind the driver were passengers gazing out at the passing scenery. It dawned on me then that maybe this was an old Habsburg type car that was pulled by horses instead of the invisible and mysterious source that powered the Chief's truck. I thought that I would have liked to ride in one if it hadn't been for those darned horse's feet that made so much racket.

Having figured all of that out, I looked up at the Chief to see if he had a ball; after all, we were on a great big expanse of grass. No such luck though. We continued on into the park and made our way to the other side where we came out onto a very busy street.

Unlike the previous ones we had been on, this one was very wide and full of cars, buses, and some very strange looking little trains that the Chief called trams. Actually, he said that the tourists called them trams, but the Viennese called them the Bim. I thought that whatever their name was, their slow trundling speed would make them great for me to ride on and sightsee.

We walked alongside the street on a very large sidewalk that had lots of people striding along it. I began to notice that I was being admired by almost everybody who saw me. I could sense them filling up with warmth and good spirits as we passed them. I heard one word many times coming from my new admirers – 'süss.' The Chief seemed to be at a loss about this word but Mom knew. She said that it was the German word for sweet. Okay! That put an extra bounce in my trot. Boy, did I love my job.

CHAPTER 11

I later found out from the Chief that the large street and sidewalk we were walking on was called the Ringstrasse, or Ring for short. He said this was yet another accomplishment of that old Habsburg guy who wanted his old city walls replaced by a big striking boulevard that encircled the old city center. I was glad to see that there were a lot of green spaces and parks mixed in amongst the very large buildings that were alongside this Ring.

It was starting to get a bit colder out, and I gave a little shiver as we walked along. Mom remarked that I should have a jacket for this weather. That made me hesitate in mid-trot. The Dude does not like clothing at all. I was glad to hear the Chief just give a noncommittal grunt in reply to her.

Back home Mom would occasionally buy clothes for us – much to her delight, not mine. My sister Daisy loves to wear clothes and has quite a wardrobe that Mom has built for her, from hoodies to snow vests and everything in between. She has no shame when it comes to parading around in whatever Mom has put on her. Me, forget it. When Mom puts clothes on The Dude, he just stands in place and refuses to move at all. I love Mom dearly and will do anything for her, but dressing me up really tests my limits.

I can always count on the Chief to be in my corner when

Anne gets the idea to adorn me with garments. Mom will always say, "Oh look how cute he looks in that." To which the Chief usually replies, "Yes, but he doesn't like that stuff on him. Give him a break and take it off him." Got to love the Chief, he can tell when I'm feeling embarrassed and tries to right the situation.

So I was really glad to hear the Chief not giving the thumbs up for clothing as we walked along the Ring. I thought to myself that that issue was now put to rest and I could relax. That was a close one for the Dude.

We eventually came to a big square that was filled with a whole bunch of little stalls. Mom said this was the Rathaus Christkindlmarkt, the largest of all Christmas markets in Vienna. She pointed out a large and graceful building behind all of the stalls and said that it was Vienna's city hall, or Rathaus. I was barely paying attention, because of all the wonderful smells that were wafting over to my nose from this place. I couldn't wait to go in!

To me it was like an open air market, kind of like the local ones we have in our town, except this one was huge and literally packed with people. There were so many that the Chief, at Mom's urging, picked me up and cradled me in his arms as we strolled in. I was glad on this occasion that Mom had him do that, because from my viewpoint on the ground, that market looked like an impenetrable wall of legs and shoes. I had already escaped nearly being trampled by horses and sure didn't want to be flattened by a herd of people!

From my new vantage point in the Chief's arms, I could now gaze across this literal sea of people who milled around the merchant's stalls. I could also see other small dogs being carried by their people. Most of them looked worried or perplexed, and glanced about very nervously. I had no such problem with being carried – I just wanted to be carried closer to the delectable smells that issued forth from many of the stalls.

It was hard to get through all of the people, and I could sense that the Chief and Mom were not going to put up with this scene for too much longer. Dad remarked to Anne that we could come back later when the place was not so crowded. Me, I wanted to hang around and get closer to some of those amazing and tantalizing smells that wafted about the market's air like a heavenly perfume.

Well, against my wishes, we headed out of the market, me craning my neck to sniff up every last scent of those wonderful aromas. Dad put me down as soon as we cleared the crowds and, after a quick sniff around to make sure nobody had dropped anything edible from the market, I trotted off with Mom and the Chief.

I noticed that this place called the Rathaus was very impressive indeed, with its high towers, arched entranceways and windows, and big clock on the highest central tower. I was pretty impressed about this building and wondered if this was another of those old Habsburg places. In the middle of my musings, the Chief picked me up and set me on a kind of picnic table that was in front of the building. What was going on now?

I soon found out when Mom, camera in hand, urged me to look at her. I knew the drill on this – she wanted me to pose.

'Okay, fine,' I thought, 'whatever makes you happy.' I gave her my best cocked head look and, after a few clicks, Mom seemed contented. My modeling job done, I jumped down from the table and got both of them headed over to a nearby park. I needed to take a break and read the local papers. Of course I had to leave a message on a small tree saying the Dude was here for any other dogs who might be doing a little reading themselves.

We walked down another cobblestone street for a bit and then stopped in front of a café. I took a deep sniff of the hearty fragrances that came from within and sighed. Much to my delight, we all went in and were shown to a table. I promptly explored underneath for any morsels that may have been dropped by the table's previous occupants. Not much was to be had, though, so I sat down and checked out the action in the restaurant from my vantage point.

Soon enough a young waitress came by and saw me. "Suss, suss." she exclaimed, and reached down to give me a nice pet and scratch behind the ears. I responded with my ears folded in enjoyment and gave a nice tail vibration. She left and returned with a bowl of water for me and some more pets. I was soaking this up when two more waitresses appeared behind her and, well, you know.

Dad said the name of the restaurant was Café Einstein, a place both he and Mom had enjoyed in past visits. From the tasty tidbits Mom and Dad gave me during the course of their lunch and all of the attention I was getting, I had to agree with them. I really liked this place! It was also very warm and cozy under that table, so I started to drift off with a smile on my face. If my siblings were able to see me right now, the cobbled streets and alleyways of Vienna would resonate with howls of indignation and injustice.

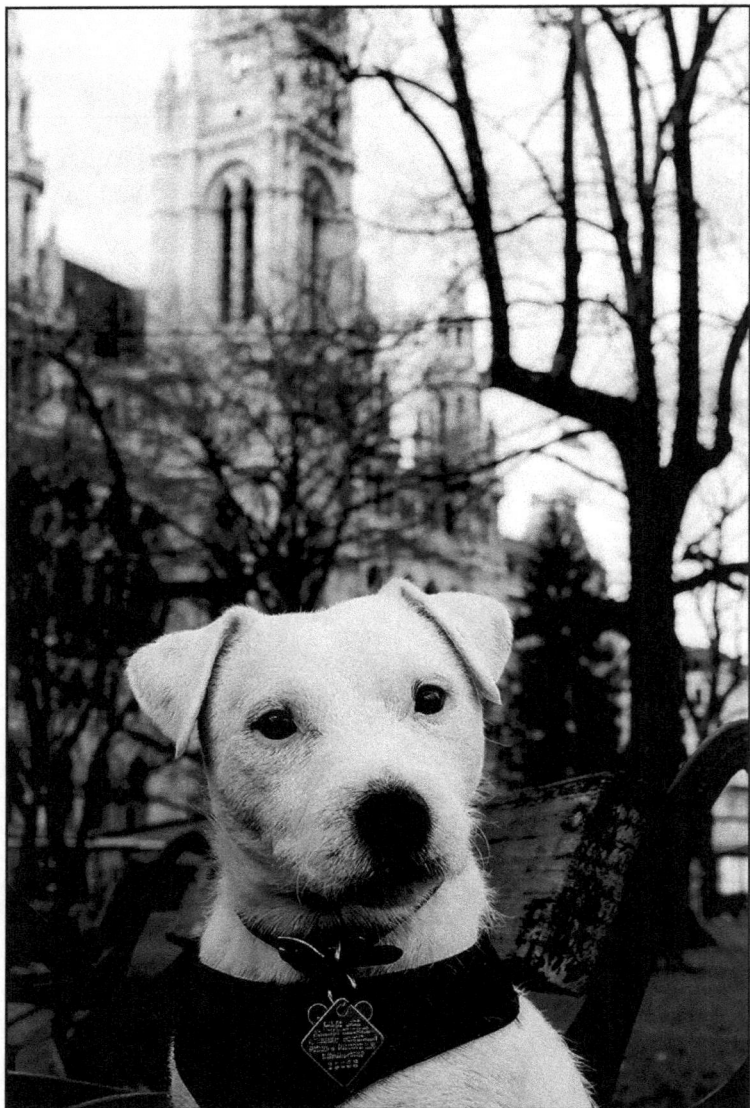

CHAPTER 12

After lunch and further adoration at the Einstein, we proceeded back to the Ring where we waited for one of those Bims to come along. The Chief and Mom were feeling a bit tired out and jet-lagged, so they wanted to go back to the apartment for a little rest. Truth be told, the Dude was feeling a little shagged himself, so I was happy to take a break as well.

In a few minutes, one of the Bims came slowly rumbling along and shuddered to a stop in front of us. I watched as Mom punched a button on the door and, with a loud click and whoosh, the door opened for us. I had to hop up a couple of stairs to get into this little train, but it was not disconcerting at all. That is until we sat down and the Chief put that vile muzzle on me again...ugh!

In spite of the monolithic contraption that weighed down my face, I liked the Bim; it was very toasty warm inside, which was very comforting to me. I also liked how nice and slow it went, so I could look out the windows at all of the many old buildings and the people bundled up in warm coats and hats as they strolled along the Ring.

From my vantage point in the Bim, I saw many dogs, their breath a visible fog in the cold, walking their moms and dads. Some had coats on, some not, but they all appeared very exultant as they trotted or pranced along. I could sense a very pleasant glow coming from both the dogs and their human parents, which made me very pleased. I love Christmastime and the wonderful feelings it brings out from everyone.

At that moment I was overcome with such gratitude and love to be here in Vienna with Mom and Dad. I wanted to emphasize my feelings by giving them both a whole lot of special licks of affection. Unfortunately, there was a big black obstruction on my muzzle that prevented me from accomplishing my goal. Still, not to lose the moment, I looked at both of them and sent pure bolts of my love at them. Hey, I was feeling so good that I even sent some of that love back to my siblings in Colorado, even Pippin.

We eventually disembarked from the Bim and, thank goodness, the black brick was again removed from my face. I was beginning to put that together now: it seemed that whenever we got on a train, be it fast or slow like the U-Bahn or Bim, I had to wear that ridiculous black mask. So it was no surprise that when we walked again down some stairs and I heard the roaring U-Bahn sounds, the plastic basket would again be attached. 'Oh well,' I thought, 'at least the rides are short and when we get off the devilish polyethylene device is removed.' It was also good to see many other dogs going through the same exact thing as me. The Dude could adjust to this routine, no problem.

We caught our U-Bahn, and it rapidly transported us back to the station near our apartment. I was getting to like the swaying of the train's car; it kind of felt like I was doing a nice bit of surfing, like I had seen humans do on television. I think I looked pretty cool, despite the black appendage attached to my face.

It was cozy and warm in the apartment, perfect for a Dude to have a bit of a nod-off and perhaps some dreams of chasing a ball. We all lay on the bed, and soon I could her the Chief's roaring snores resonating around the room – until Mom gave him a nudge, that is. Very soon the warmth and relative quiet made me drift off into a pleasant sleep.

I awoke feeling very nice and drowsy, but I had to make a visit outside to take care of some things, so with a nice stretch, I got up. I didn't need to do any urging for the Chief to get up this time – he was on it. We went out for a bit, and after we came back to the apartment Mom gave me an early dinner, which was a nice treat. Love Mom, she always takes good care of me!

We went back out in the late afternoon. Dad said we were going to meet some people at another Christmas market. Mom said that it had been close to seven years since they had seen Monika and Peter, whom, she said, lived in Vienna. Well, I was up for that, because I always love to meet new people.

After another short ride on the U-Bahn – yes, with the plastic lead weight on – we arrived back in the old city. We walked along the Ring again, but this time we headed in a different direction away from where we had been earlier in the day. I was a bit disappointed, because I remembered the wonderful smells of that Rathaus Christmas market and wished to return for possible treats. 'Oh well.' I thought, 'Maybe wherever we are headed will have something similar to offer a little Jack.'

We wandered a bit around the Ring area, and it seemed that Mom and Dad were looking for something specific. It was raining lightly and kind of cold, but I was up for whatever the Chief and Mom wanted to do, even if it was getting lost amongst the big buildings surrounding the Ring. I wasn't detecting any food smells around here, though, and was hoping we might eventually end up at that market or a café again.

We stopped in front of a small shop that had an essence around the doorway that spoke to me of many dogs happily crossing its threshold. Mom said it was a pet boutique that had special things for dogs. Ha! I knew it was a pet shop from the smell, no need to tell me. As we entered the shop, I thought this must mean I would be getting some special treats bought for me, or perhaps a nice toy that squeaked when I bit it. We were greeted by a nice saleslady who spoke to Mom in German. Mom asked her a question in that same language, and with a nod the lady took us down an aisle to what I hoped would be a nice display of toys.

Imagine my surprise when we ended up in front of the dog clothing rack. I was totally thunderstruck! The Dude had been caught totally unawares, and now there was no escape. I looked up at the Chief with accusing eyes, but he avoided my baleful glare and pretended to be investigating cat toys. Darn! I sighed and resigned myself for what was to come. I still had hope, though, that either nothing would be in my size or that the Chief would regain his senses and bail me out.

It seemed like I spent hours enduring hundreds of articles being fitted on me, each one accompanied by a chorus of oohs and ahhs from Mom and the darned saleslady. Finally Mom decided that I was going to get an Italian made raincoat. I didn't like it much at all and refused to walk around the store in it, but that did not stop Mom's single minded purpose – I was going to have a coat no matter what. The Chief did raise his eyebrows when he saw the price, and for one fleeting moment I had a glimmer of hope that I might escape this terrible fate. That was soon dashed as he reached for his wallet and paid the saleslady. In my mind I could hear Pippin laughing with unbridled glee.

Reluctantly and with more than a few tugs on my leash, I walked out of the store wearing the coat. I kept looking up at the Chief with my most mournful looks, hoping he would soon take pity on me and remove it. No such luck. We soon boarded another Bim – plastic face mask reattached – and off we went.

We ended up at a smaller version of the Rathaus market, but it still had many exotic and enticing odors that made my mouth begin to water. Dad said this was the market on Maria Theresa square. He said that Maria Theresa was another of those old Habsburgs and that there was a statue of her here. I really wasn't too interested in all of that; I just wanted to go investigate those smells in the market. I even forgot that I was wearing that darned jacket.

This market was not as full of people as the earlier one, so I was able to trot in on my four little paws. You might say that instead of trotting around with my head up, it became more like a shuffling walk with my nose carefully sniffing everything in my path. Being on the ground gave me the opportunity to spy out any dropped morsels for quick consumption before Mom or the Chief noticed. I did find more than a few little delicacies to quickly gulp; there's nothing like some tasty treats after dinner to make the Dude happy.

I perceived so much warm conviviality in this market. Lots of people were greeting each other in very good-natured spirits. Others were sitting and conversing at small tables in front of the stalls. Many were having drinks of what Dad called Punsch – a special alcoholic concoction made for the holidays – and eating all manner of fine smelling items. Smiles were in abundance everywhere, which of course increased when I was noticed. The atmosphere made me pause from my snuffling. To me, it felt like a warm dog blanket of peace and well-being had seemingly settled on this market, if not the whole of Vienna itself. I loved this sense of peaceful camaraderie and wished that it could be maintained by people the world over all the time, not just at Christmas.

I picked up the pace a bit, for I could feel something or somebody was up ahead waiting for us. I zeroed in on two people standing in front of a large statue and knew that this must be Peter and Monika. Moments later my feeling was confirmed as the Chief and Mom walked up to greet them. Of course I was admired by Monika and Peter who remarked again and again how handsome I was. I gave them the whole hitch-walk, complete with tail vibration, and my ears folded back in pure enjoyment.

Soon enough we all went wandering amongst the merchants stalls so Mom and Dad could maybe do some shopping. Me, I returned to the job at hand, nose riveted to the ground, in search of any more delectable bits that had been dropped. During the course of my nibbling, I noticed other dogs in the market doing the same thing. I didn't feel jealous though; there were plenty of savory tidbits for all to enjoy.

Eventually we all left the market and headed out through the streets of Vienna. It was quite dark by now and a cold drizzle was descending on the city. I was secretly glad to have that jacket on now – it was pretty snug and warm. There was no way I would ever let Alex and Anne know that, though; it would set a bad precedent. I did have some pretty cold paws and ears and longed for a little break somewhere warm.

My wish was soon granted as we came to another heavenly smelling restaurant and entered. I trotted right in this time, secure in the knowledge that the Dude was welcome in Viennese eating establishments. I settled in under our table, knowing the drill now, and soon a dish of water was brought along with, well, you know, smiles, pets, etc. It gets kind of hard to keep saying how much I was being admired: I do not want to come off as a snob; I am just doing what I was put on this Earth for. I must say Vienna was really fertile ground for me to work, that's for sure.

Mom and the Chief's dinners were very good indeed, as I can attest to from the fine samples given to me as I lay under the table. They talked a lot with Monika and Peter about Vienna's history and what it was like to live in the city. From what I could sense and smell, our new friends were, unbelievable as it may seem, cat people. Well, I forgave them for this because they were so nice and I could tell they had really kind hearts. Maybe if I hung around them long enough, they might see the error of their ways.

After dinner, we all said our goodbyes to Monika and Peter, in which I was rewarded with some nice pets and scratches behind the ears. This of course made me do another round of hitch-walk and a bit of prancing about from pure joy. It was still wet and getting colder, so we made our way to the nearest U-Bahn station and zipped back to our nice warm apartment. I settled in and drifted off to dreamland.

CHAPTER 13

I again had to wake Alex early in the morning with my little song and scratch routine. We went outside and, after an extensive reading of the neighborhood papers, I took care of business, leaving more news for the next dog to read. When we returned, Anne had the coffee on and, most importantly, my breakfast laid out and ready for me. I trotted over and took in the fine aroma of it before digging in. I was getting used to the idea that no siblings that would be standing around, gazing at me with feigned hunger expressions on their well-fed faces. The Dude was now able to take a little time to savor and relish his food.

After breakfast the Chief said that since this was Christmas Eve we would have to shop for food and such. He said that in Vienna all the stores close early for the holiday and remain closed for a couple of days afterwards, so we needed to stock up. I thought that was very cool for the people here to be able to have days off to spend with their families, and their dogs, of course.

Instead of grabbing my leash, the Chief put on his coat and slipped out the door before I could react. This was inconceivable to me – I always got to go with the Chief! As the front door closed on him, I began a mournful howling song of injustice and sorrow, directed at Mom and the room in general. Life can be so unfair to a dog at times. When at last the Chief returned, I had a nice hitch-walk dance around the apartment and forgave him immediately. I would keep an eye on him in the future, though, no more of that slipping away without me stuff!

The day went pretty much like our first day: we took the U-Bahn into the old city and walked around the big Rathaus Christmas market. I had to be carried again due to the herds of people who were perusing the market. I was betting that there was a lot of nice stuff on the ground for me to sample, but I was happy to be carried safely above all of those tramping feet.

After a while we left the market and headed over to another park where I gratefully left a few Christmas messages for my fellow dogs. In this particular park was a large golden statue of a man with a violin poised to play. Dad said he was Johann Strauss, the Waltz King. I knew of him because Dad and Mom had often told the tale of how they had met each other and fallen in love while singing in the chorus of one of his operas. Dad also played a lot of his music at home, and all of us dogs really were soothed by the light and lilting melodies that drifted like magic through the air. Mom had the Chief and I stand in front of old Johann for some pictures, with me striking some very noble poses. I could imagine Pippin, when he finally saw these shots, looking at me and snorting with jealousy.

We wrapped things up later in the afternoon because Mom said we were attending a special Christmas Eve dinner in a few hours. As we made our way back to the apartment, I sensed immense excitement and anticipation coming off of all of the people we passed. Yes, Christmas with all of its good will and fellowship, was very near. I was very happy about all of this, and even when the Chief put the muzzle on me, my spirit was not dampened in the least bit.

It was late evening and pretty cold when we departed for our dinner. Dad said we were going to a restaurant called Der Kuckuck. He said it was a very elegant establishment and so I would need to be extra courteous and respectful while there. Of course, I knew that this would be no problem for the Dude, he adjusts and knows how to act in literally every situation.

In spite of being told about the place, I was really surprised when we got there. Der Kuckuck – The Cuckoo in English – was really classy. We were met inside by a gracious man in a nice suit who led us past white linen draped tables with warm flickering candles upon them. The soft light of the candles illuminated the convivial faces of people who I could sense were anticipating a really good meal. Of course, the exclamations of joy at the sight of me were many and in a host of different languages as well. That made me prance along even more jauntily. I placed myself under our table, and soon a nice dish of water was brought to me. Ahh, these Viennese really knew how treat a dog on holiday. Now, if they just would learn to bring out some tender morsels with the water, life would be perfect.

One thing you notice as a dog, especially if you are lying under a table at a restaurant, is people's shoes. During the past few days, I had seen quite a few pairs from my under-the-table vantage point. Most of the places we had gone to the shoes and boots were relatively ordinary for this time of year and climate. The footwear I saw on the Kuckuck's patrons looked to be very formal and stylish – nothing ordinary here. I wondered how they would fare outside in the cold and wet. I sure was glad I did not have to suffer putting my four paws into such things. Nope, barefoot paws that can be licked clean in a jiffy; that was for me.

Under a table close by I spotted another dog who was looking right back at me with his head raised a little off his paws. We regarded each other warily for a few moments, but in the spirit of the season and the fact there were probably enough table treats to go around, we both silently accepted a truce for the evening.

Mom and Dad's dinner smelled very good indeed. It was served in many courses, of which I had a little sampling of each. Did I mention it was great to be the only dog on a holiday? The whole dining experience took longer than what I had recently become used to, so being as how I was in a linen draped and warm dark spot under the table, I drifted off.

I had a dream about living back up in the mountains of Colorado. I had awakened in the middle of the night to a chorus of coyote howls, if you want to call them howls. Coyotes, when together at night, make more of a bizarre laughing sound that always makes the hair on my back stand up. The howls seemed at first quite a bit away, but, after a short interval of quiet, a burst of the hysterical ululations came from what seemed right outside our window. Then came a furious series of slams against the front door, as if bodies were hurling themselves at it to gain egress. I pawed desperately at the Chief and Mom, but they would not stir. I leapt to the floor and ran into the living room, placing myself squarely in front of the door, which was starting to give way. A little shakily, I set my face in a fearsome grin of rage and braced myself for the coming onslaught.

I growled awake, to find myself safe and warm, still under the table at the Kuckuck. Whew! Mom reached down and gave me a nice reassuring stroke, followed by a nice tidbit from her plate. I had a little drink of water and relaxed again, very glad that I was in Vienna and not facing a pack of those marauding coyote fiends.

After dinner, we walked along the uneven stone cobbles toward a U-Bahn station. The city had become very quiet, and Mom and Dad's footsteps echoed off the old buildings and down the narrow alleyways. A light snow had begun to fall, and like a shimmering white veil it dusted rooftops, statues, and monuments. As we passed an old church, there issued forth the sound of a chorus singing something very soothing and beautiful. The church's high stained-glass windows were magically illuminated by the flickering of all of the candles from within. I told myself to remember this scene and try to describe it to Daisy, she would really be able to appreciate the solemn grace of it all.

There were very few people about the city and on the U-Bahn as we made our way home. I guessed that was because it was Christmas Eve and everyone was home with their families. Dad had said that in Austria, Christmas Eve was when everybody celebrated, unlike our home in Colorado where Christmas day was when all of the action was. I wondered what Daisy and the rest back at home would be doing on Christmas without Mom and Dad. I hoped that Grandma would do something special for them.

CHAPTER 14

Well, the next few days became a nice routine for all of us. I'd get Mom and the Chief up so I could go outside and read the local news. I would always leave some messages of my own as well. Mom would have a delicious breakfast waiting for me when I returned, and then we would all go out to catch the U-Bahn to the old city.

We would walk around visiting different neighborhoods, and any time we came to a monument, or old piece of architecture, I would be posed and pictures taken. One special place we went to was an amusement park called the Prater, where I was stationed in front of a great big wheel with cars attached to it. Dad explained it was a Ferris wheel called the Riesenrad, made famous by being in a movie called The Third Man. I was more interested in all the messages left by the dogs in this area, but I gave the Chief a smile and a tail vibration to humor him.

Once again we visited with Monika and Peter and also a former student of Anne's who lived over near the Prater amusement park. The admirations and looks of joy when I was spotted anywhere in the city became a very nice routine – I felt I was really doing some major work here in Vienna.

I became so used to Vienna that even the loud clattering of the horse drawn old Habsburg cars rocking along the cobblestones did not bother me as much. Traveling on all of the public transit was now a piece of dog biscuit, I knew the drill for being a good rider. I even forgot about the black plastic hindrance on my face when we rode. As we walked the streets, I would nod at most of the other dogs we passed in casual greeting. All in all, I was beginning to feel like a real big city dog, and, to tell the truth, I kind of liked it.

As we were getting close to the end of our visit, the Chief asked Mom if she would like to make a trip to another city. He said the name of this city was Salzburg and that it was up in the mountains of Austria. I thought that would be a nice change to see somewhere else, and Mom agreed as well.

We all got up early, and, after all of our morning routines, made our way via the U-Bahn to the Westbahnhof train station. The station seemed to me like a smaller version of an airport, so at first I was a little nervous until I saw that there were big trains lined up at various platforms. Though I had not been on a full sized train, I felt that it would be another piece of biscuit after the U-Bahn.

Dad and Mom puzzled over the ticket machine for a bit but finally figured it out. I got my own half price second class ticket for the journey. I felt very important having my own ticket – nothing like this ever occurred at home. Of course, I had to don the plastic misery again, but, as I said before, I was getting used to that.

When we came up to it, the train was pretty big and had a lot more cars than the U-Bahn, but I was not in the least deterred by that. When we reached the proper car, I happily jumped up its stairs – a new adventure! I liked the inside of this train; it had plenty of windows and nice seats where I could sit on Mom's lap and gaze out. A whistle blew, and the train gently lurched forward along the tracks – we were off!

The train rolled along and in a very short while, the large buildings of Vienna gave way to beautiful green rolling countryside. I looked longingly out of the window at the verdant fields, wishing I could go do a fine long romp through them. The sight caused me to think of the nice green grass back home and, of course, a ball game with the Chief. I felt a twinge of homesickness right then and wondered how Daisy and the rest of my siblings were doing.

Sitting in the warmth of Anne's lap, I soon drifted off to a nice sleep that was only slightly broken by the few quick stops the train made along the way. At one point I woke to see the train conductor checking my ticket. He smiled at me and reached down to give me a little scratch behind the ear and along my back. I could tell he was a dog person because he knew just the right places to touch on. He gave a wink at Mom and the Chief with a gesture that said it was okay to take off the muzzle. Oh yeah, he was definitely a dog person!

I looked out the window again and saw that we were now going through a forested area, which made me wonder if there were any Austrian squirrels to possibly chase. I certainly had not seen any in the parks of Vienna, but I figured that with all of the dogs in the city, they would probably stay well-hidden in the trees. Out in the forest I thought there were probably a lot of them, maybe even some of those arrogant foxes were out there as well.

The train began an upward ascent into more mountainous

and forested territory. I was really beginning to appreciate this country, for sure. I had no idea such a wonderland existed outside of Vienna. I really wished we could get off for a while, so I could have some sniffs of the lush mountain forest and perhaps a little fox chase as well.

Eventually we broke out of the forest and began descending down into sort of a valley. I could see that we were coming up on another city, but not as big as Vienna. I could see old towers and spires from churches towards the center of the city. The buildings on the outskirts were of a more modern architecture, as if they had grown up around the old center. The entire city was ringed by snowcapped mountains that had a very nice glow from the late afternoon sun.

What really caught my eyes, though, was a great castle that sat on a small mountain. This huge fortress-like structure overlooked the entire city, as if it were some benign being keeping watch over all of the inhabitants who lived below it. The effect of the sun reflecting off of its high walls and towers made it by far the most majestic thing I had seen so far in Austria – I was really impressed.

The Chief said that the city was Salzburg and was where we were going to get off. That made me very excited because it looked like a fun place for me to explore and strut my stuff. I also needed to find a little grass to take care of some personal business and read the local papers.

The train came to a stop at the station, and we disembarked, quickly making our way outside. Luckily for me, there was a small park-like area to visit right across from the station. It was pretty warm outside, so after doing my thing and getting some sniffs in I plopped down and had a nice stretch on the sun-warmed grass.

At the Chief's urging and a few tugs on my leash, I finally got up and started to walk with him and Anne towards the center of the city. Salzburg was a pretty busy little city with lots of people going about their daily business, hurrying here and there along the sidewalks. Even so, most of those who saw me trotting along smiled and began to emanate that familiar inner warmth of joy. The Dude was spreading the love to Salzburg now, even though I had been here less than an hour!

After a little bit, we turned off the large street we had been following onto a smaller cobblestone street. This street was lined with older buildings that reflected the sunlight making it so warm that the Chief took off his coat and I began to pant a little. I had not had any water since Vienna and was getting pretty thirsty. I hoped we would reach our destination soon.

Within a few blocks we arrived at what the Chief called Hotel Auersperg. It was pretty nondescript on the outside, but when we entered the place my eyes widened considerably. The lobby area had lots of polished wood and gleaming granite floors. All of the people who worked there were very smartly dressed and quite professional looking. I had seen places like this before when Mom and Dad were watching travel shows. It was what Mom called a boutique hotel and seemed very classy to my little eyes.

The man who was at the reception desk greeted us warmly and gave me a huge smile. After the Chief did all of the paperwork for the room, the man looked at me with another smile and said, "And for you my little man, we have included a few special things in the room." That lit me up – I couldn't wait to see what lay in store for me.

We made our way up soft carpeted stairs to our room, and the Chief let me off my leash to explore. I hurriedly sniffed around to find what special things might be there for me. I looked and looked around the rooms and balcony hoping to get a whiff of a nice exotic treat for me, but nothing turned up. Then Mom pointed to some items near the front entranceway. Quickly I ran over to see what the hotel had left for me. What I discovered was a large dog dish and nice warm blanket. I was a little disappointed, but at the same time I felt very important at the thought of those things being left just for me.

After we unpacked, we went out to explore Salzburg. The sun was getting lower on the horizon but still bathed us in some warmth. We walked along some narrow cobbled streets and eventually came out to a bridge that spanned a large river. Slowly, we made our way across the bridge – Mom making me pose at various points along the way – and came to the older part of Salzburg.

I could sense that the buildings here were very old indeed, not like the mostly rebuilt structures in Vienna. Looking up as I walked along the narrow streets, I could see spires and towers reaching towards the evening sky majestically. All of the buildings had very unique and interesting signs that hung from them. Some of the lanes were decorated with very pretty Christmas decorations that dangled above like so many tiny multi-colored stars.

The streets were very crowded with shoppers and sight-seers, so I had to be constantly on the watch for people who weren't paying attention to where they were stepping. Even so, I trotted happily along, basking in the many adoring looks and exclamations of admiration directed at me.

We walked and explored, pausing now and again to look into the many shop windows displaying their wares. One in particular was a very nice smelling bakery, which had all kinds of sweet looking treats in their window. I hoped we would go in so I could indulge in furthering my gastronomical education, but no such luck. Sometimes I think the Chief and Mom need to cock their heads and listen to the thoughts I direct at them more.

The sky began to darken, and Salzburg began to light up in a very magical way. Along with the decorations lighting the streets, all of the shops, restaurants, and cafes had nice old looking lamps outside their doors, which beckoned with their warmth to come inside. As the sun set, it began to get really cold. I amazed myself by thinking I would like to have my jacket on right then. That was a first!

Eventually we found ourselves in front of a small restaurant that looked really cozy and inviting from the outside. When we entered, we were greeted by a lady who, of course, looked upon me and...you know. She told Mom and Dad that all of the tables were booked and she was sorry. Just as we were turning to leave, another lady came in from the dining area and told us that a family there would love to share their table with us. I guessed they must have seen me and my magic had worked on them.

The family greeted us in German and gave me lots of pets with many compliments. I gave them some ears and a lot of tail vibrations then settled under the table. It was nice and warm in this restaurant, so I hoped Mom and Dad would take their time. I was surprised when the waitress brought me not only a dish of water but a delicious treat as well. Ah, warmth, water, admiration, and treats: what a great time I was having here!

More people came in to eat while we were there. I perked up when I saw a shaggy dog come in with his people and plop gratefully under their table. We eyed each other for a few seconds and then went back to our own business. We had silently agreed that this warm place was big enough for both of us. With good will in my heart, I returned my gaze up to Mom and Dad in expectation of treats from the table.

After dinner, we walked back through the old town and perused more shop windows. A very chill wind began to blow off of the river, which again made me wish for my jacket. Miraculously, Mom produced it from her bag, and soon I was bundled up very nicely. I still walked as though I did not like it, though – it wouldn't do to give Mom the idea that the Dude was getting accustomed to clothes.

It was getting late, and the shops were all now mostly closed, so we walked back to our hotel and our nice warm room. The bed in our room had the best kind of covers that were soft and filled with what Mom said were goose feathers. I loved acting like a wild dog and frisking in them. It was pure joy and also entertained the Chief and Mom to no end. Nothing like a good frisk before bedtime!

Morning came, and I awoke to see that Dad had gotten up before me and was now urging me to hop to it so we could go outside for some paper-reading. We went down to the hotel's garden area, which had a lot of news from other dogs who had visited there. Most interesting sniffs indeed, but the overwhelming aroma I picked up was coming from the breakfast room. I hurried through my routines, hoping we would be heading in the direction of those heavenly fragrances.

The breakfast room smelled even better when I was positioned beneath our table there. I sniffed all kinds of meats, eggs, and some things I was unfamiliar with. I was definitely up for any new gourmet adventures, though, and hoped the Chief would slip me some for my edification. The Chief and Mom came through big time, and I enjoyed many tasty morsels that put my taste buds into a state of nirvana. Oh, I liked this hotel very much indeed!

After breakfast, we went back to our room. I was disappointed to see that Mom and Dad began to pack up their cases. Darn, I wanted to stay here for at least a week or more. Mom did say that she sure would like to return here for a longer stay, which bucked up my spirits a bit.

We left the hotel and walked back to the train station. I wondered where we would end up this time. I found myself now enjoying the idea of being surprised by stepping off a conveyance like the train or U-Bahn to find myself in a totally new environment. This was a great adventure!

Like a seasoned pro, I hopped aboard the train and settled in on Mom's lap. I was ready to go on to more fun! Soon the train began to slowly click-clack out of the station and rapidly picked up the pace to where the scenery went by like a shot. Being as how the Dude had been there and done that, I drifted off for a nice long nap.

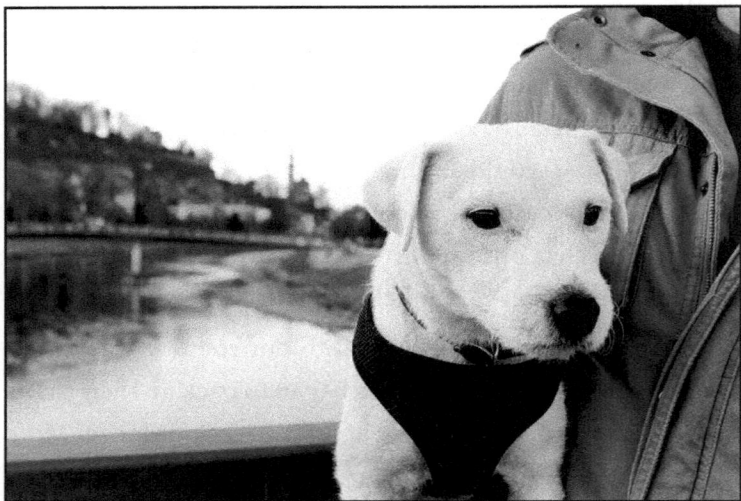

CHAPTER 15

When I awoke, the clacking and clicking of the train was slowing down. I stretched, gave Mom a nice little lick on the face, and looked out the window. No more green countryside was in evidence now; we were surrounded by buildings again. As the pace of the train began to slow to a crawl, I began to recognize some of the structures. We were back in Vienna again!

We retraced the route we had taken the day before back to our apartment. I was a little disappointed that we had not arrived at another new destination, but I figured we would go out again and wander the streets of Vienna and there would be new sniffs for me. I settled in on the bed and waited for the Chief and Anne.

While I was sprawled out on the covers, I heard the Chief ask Anne what shops we should go to for buying gifts to bring back home. He sat looking at me for a moment and said, "Well Dude, this is it. Tomorrow morning we fly back home." I could sense more than a little sadness coming from the old Chief when he said this, but there was also a bit of anticipation as well. It was if he did not want to leave but felt homesick for Colorado and our life there. I jumped down from the bed and hopped into his lap, giving him lots of reassuring kisses. The Dude never likes it when the Chief or Mom are feeling low and will do his utmost to cheer them up.

We spent the evening going to many shops and purchasing small items for people back home. I did my job very well, leaving the shopkeepers smiling and glowing inside. Thank goodness we did not go to any pet boutiques!

I began to get a little sad myself at the thought of leaving Vienna and going home. I think I might have even endured another visit to a pet boutique and let Mom indulge in making me try on clothes, if it meant we could stay longer. We walked by one of the Christmas markets, which, now that the holiday was over, was dark and deserted. That made me sad too. It was almost as if Vienna was telling us that the party was over and now it was time to leave.

After a quiet dinner, we went back to our apartment, and Mom began to pack everything up for the journey back. The landlady, Beatrix, came by to make sure all was okay. I went over to her and gave her a big grin and tail vibration, and rubbed up against her. One last flirtation in Vienna!

Very early in the morning, the Chief took me out for one last stroll so I could leave some farewell messages to the dogs of the neighborhood. I hoped the Dude would be remembered by them for a long time to come as that upstart American Jack who came to stay for a while.

Back at the apartment, I was a little miffed when Mom and Dad ate some breakfast but did not give me my usual delicious Viennese wet food. The Chief caught my look of disbelief and said, "Sorry, Dude, you are flying today, so no food." I looked over at Mom, who smiled and gave me a slice of some meat from the table, saying "Well, at least not a full meal. Don't want you to get sick or mess your crate." I thought, 'The Dude mess his crate? C'mon Mom, who do you think I am, Pippin?'

After their breakfast – and my pauper's meal – Mom and Dad lugged the bags down to the street, where we were met by a taxi driver. Once again I was put into my crate and loaded in the back of the van. Of course I was not too happy about that, but I resigned myself to my fate and lay down for a doze.

When we arrived at the airport, I began to realize that I was going to undergo another bout with the big birds. The thought of this made me a little apprehensive and nervous, but at least this time I knew what to expect. The Chief leashed me and led me around the outside of the airport for a final relief break. This time, knowing what was to come, I took full advantage of a small grassy area and left another little message for those dogs who would be arriving or departing.

The lady at the counter inside gave me a warm smile and told Mom and Dad she wanted to keep me. Mom and Dad both laughed and shook their heads, and I gave her a very flirtatious grin with my ears folded in delight. That really made her glow from within, and it cheered me up as well.

The Chief looked at me and gestured for me to hop inside the crate, which I reluctantly did. Mom and the Chief both reached in and gave me some farewell pets before I was wheeled away. I could feel that they were very anxious and worried about me. I wished I could tell them that I would be all right, that the big birds would not eat me. I decided I would send them loving thoughts once they were on the bird with me so they would feel better.

As the sun began to rise, I was loaded onto one of those small trucks and shuttled to the feet of the big steel bird. I sighed to myself and settled in for the long voyage home.

CHAPTER 16

The return was much the same as the outgoing journey. This time, however, with my previous experience, I was a bit more relaxed. After our first stop, where I was loaded on the bigger steel bird, I pretty much slept and dreamed of home and siblings.

I awoke suddenly when the bird jolted in contact with the ground. I wondered if this was the last stop or would there be more. I hoped this was it, because I really had to take care of some business outside of the crate!

Soon after that bird rolled to a stop, its belly was opened, and I was offloaded into a dazzling sunny day. With one whiff of the outside air, I knew where I was – home! I began to get really excited, knowing I would soon be reunited with Mom and the Chief.

After being put on another truck and brought inside of a big building, I was wheeled into another room with those roundish contraptions moving bags around them. Out of a crowd of people, Mom and the Chief appeared, all smiles and happiness when they spotted me. Soon I was leashed and out of the crate, giving them both butt wiggles and many kisses. We had all made it back, and I was a very happy Dude!

Before we could leave the room, a man in a uniform asked for my USDA papers. The Chief gave them to him, and he scrutinized the pages for a bit before nodding and handing them back. He then looked at me and smiled, saying, "Welcome back to the USA!" With that we all walked out with our luggage in tow, down a corridor and through some doors, which revealed Grandma waiting with a big smile. Ears, wiggles, rubs, licks, and a quick hitch-walk of joy for Grandma!

I was very happy to get out of the airport and over to the little dog park outside so I could unleash a torrent of stored up...well, you know. After that we all piled into Grandma's car and drove out of the airport garage. Grandma talked and talked about a great snowfall that had happened after we left for Vienna and also asked many questions about our trip. Time passed pretty fast and, very soon it seemed, we arrived home.

I hopped out of the car and could hear the familiar excited barks and howls coming from our house. Oh, yeah, I was back for sure. When the Chief opened the door, all hell broke loose. Everybody rushed out of the house to greet us – well, mainly the Chief and Mom, but I got some welcomes from Daisy.

I kind of hung back as everyone went up the stairs to the living room. I was no longer the special only dog, which made me feel pretty sad. Just then the Chief came back down the stairs, sat down on the first one and looked into my eyes for a moment. He said, "Dude, you were the best on that trip. You know that? I just want you to know that you are always number one in my eyes." He looked at me one more time, gave me a wink and said, "Okay my man, ready to go get 'em?" I was brimming with love for him right then and gave him a big lick on the face. Together we went up the stairs to face the barking fray.

After all the excitement settled down a bit, Pipsqueak came over and tried to assert himself in front of me. Ha, with a low growl and a show of my teeth, he backed off real quick. I presented my rear end to him, and he sulkily walked away. The Dude was back and had retaken his throne!

Later that night, I lay awake and found myself remembering how as a young pup I had hated to go out of the house for walks. Mom or the Chief would have to pull me along until I finally gave in and reluctantly walked with them. When we drove anywhere, I would grunt, whimper, and complain the whole time I was in the vehicle.

Somewhere along the line, I changed and went from a reluctant to an eager walker. I loved going in the car or truck now and joyfully hung my head out the window for sniffs. Even before this trip, I was eager to just go somewhere out of the house and yard. I thought maybe it was part of my growing up process. Either way, I was really different now.

Lying next to the Chief, I went over the trip we had taken and thought how much I had experienced. Earlier, I had tried to tell Daisy and the others about it while we were out in the backyard on patrol, but they just looked at me in disbelief. They couldn't begin to understand what I was talking about with big steel birds, flying, U-Bahns and the like. Nor could they fathom the concept of being in a foreign land. I finally gave up. What good was it to try and describe all of this to dogs who felt going to a foreign land was like going camping!

Lily and Pippin had given me sniffs of derision and

gone haughtily trotting back into the house, but Daisy had remained behind and regarded me for a moment. I could hear her thoughts telling me to give it up and just be happy that I was home and needed to look no further than our backyard for adventure. She had then walked off towards the house. I sighed and began to follow but then heard a noise from above. I looked up to see something that before had mystified me, but not now. It was a big steel bird majestically making its way across the sky.

As I drifted off to sleep, I thought that, no, it was never going to be the same for me again. How could the backyard be enough for a dog who had flown in the belly of a big bird and survived, lived for a time in a foreign city, and had all of the other adventures I had experienced? Now, when I saw those big birds up in the sky, I would wonder what exotic destinations they were heading to. I finally slept and dreamed of cobblestone streets, the clip-clopping of leather clad horses, and old Habsburgs.

Yes, I was home, but in my mind I was up in the clouds, flying off to see what was over the next horizon, exploring with new eyes and spreading joy to people all over the world.

EPILOGUE

Winter turned to early spring, and I settled back into the usual routine. Crows were chased, squirrels repelled back into the trees, and ball games were had. I sometimes would look up and catch a glimpse of the big birds, and it would fill me with a little bit of longing. But still, life was good and The Dude was happy.

Sometimes Mom and Dad would watch travel programs with us. This was special to me because there was an unspoken thought between the three of us that we had done something magical together. They knew that I was appreciating what they were watching while my siblings just kind of hung out. The Chief would usually look and me and make a comment about how I had been such a great traveler, followed by a knowing wink. I liked that. The Chief and I always had a special bond, and traveling together had only made it stronger.

One day the Chief told me to come on and get into the truck, because we had something important to do. I immediately jumped to it, because the Chief wasn't getting any younger and needed his sharp-eyed navigator to keep an ever-vigilant watch. The Dude always looks after the Chief! As we drove along, I could sense a vibe coming off him that felt vaguely familiar, but I couldn't quite place it. 'Oh well,' I thought, 'it must not be that important.'

After a bit, we pulled up in front of one of my most favorite places, the pet store! After we got out of the truck, the Chief turned, gave me a wink and a big smile, and said, "Okay, Dude, we have to go in and get you some new equipment for our trip to Austria and Italy this coming August. This time you are going to fly with us, not in a crate. What do you say to that?" Hitch-walk, tail vibration, ears, and yeehaw!

AUTHOR'S NOTE

After three more trips to Europe, Thor finally retired after his last trip to Germany, Austria, and Italy. The Dude was the best traveling companion one could ever hope for, always up for any challenge. He passed away early in 2024 after 15 wonderful years with us. We miss him terribly. There will never be another such as he.

ABOUT THE AUTHOR

Alex Starke lives with his wife, Anne, and four Jack Russell terriers in Eugene, Oregon. He is a graduate of the University of Oregon with a degree in Medieval Studies and a minor in Early Modern European History. He currently is doing fine art photography and just living the dream.

Thor wanted all of his of his readers to be aware that there are many Jack Russell terriers out there that need good homes. He urges you to adopt from a State or local Jack Russell rescue agency where there are lots of great Jacks looking for people with kind and open hearts.

www.ingramcontent.com/pod-product-compliance
Lightning Source LLC
Chambersburg PA
CBHW060820050426
42449CB00008B/1745